The Foundation for a Successful Life

Golden Truths for Personal & Family Growth

VOLUME 1

By

Joseph Hyacinthe Jr.

The Foundation for a Successful Life
Golden Truths for Personal & Family Growth

Volume 1

Paperback

Joseph Hyacinthe Jr.

ISBN: 979-8-9940810-3-7

To my mother,

who wasn't there to raise me, but taught me the

power of prayer, family, and love.

Table Of Contents

Acknowledgements

I want to start by expressing my heartfelt gratitude to my wonderful wife, Marie. Her feedback and insights have significantly enhanced many aspects of this book. Her unwavering support, love, and caring spirit from the very beginning have been crucial in helping me reach this important milestone. Thank you so much, my love. To my two amazing sons, Nathan and Noah, you have inspired me to become a better father. Without you, I would not have gained the wisdom I have today, nor would I have been able to write this book. Caring for, protecting, and providing for you has shown me the true meaning of life and allowed me to experience the power of God and His blessings in countless ways. Thank you, boys! Dad loves you.

I also want to thank my mother, who inspires me to push myself and has been the best spiritual role model I could ever ask for. Without her, I would not have the beautiful and amazing life I have today. She taught me to hold on to God during challenging times and to never give up. Witnessing her faith in God has been a remarkable experience. Thank you, Mom.

To my brother Anobb and his family, who have steadfastly supported their loved ones despite facing their own challenges: your strength and commitment to family have profoundly impacted my life. Your support, advice, and our evening conversations have brought comfort to my soul and lightened my days. I love you, brother.

Lastly, to my sister Cecile, who shares similar struggles and consistently encourages others to see the brighter side of life: your laughter and uplifting spirit are truly unique. Your hugs have transformed a significant part of my life, helping me appreciate the little things that bring greater peace and joy.

Introduction

Have you ever felt beaten or broken? Have you experienced abuse, coercion, cheating, or being taken advantage of? Moreover, do you sometimes feel that everything is working against you and that you can't seem to win? Have you also felt lost, confused, and frustrated, uncertain about what to do next? If you answered yes to any of these questions, then this collection of books is for you.

As this is the first volume of a much larger series, it will reveal eleven important truths that many people are unaware of or have yet to master. Consequently, you will gain a clear understanding of each situation and its impact on you and those around you. Additionally, you will discover valuable guidance on how to address or overcome some of the most challenging issues that have troubled millions of people for years. Therefore, stay tuned!

I used to believe that being a Christian meant allowing people to walk all over me and take advantage of my kindness, believing that God would take care of those individuals and bless me for my generosity. I also thought I had to forgive people seventy times seven, even when they showed me disrespect. But can you really do that? Can you let others mistreat you repeatedly without standing up for yourself? If you think the answer is yes, then some of the topics discussed in the following series may not resonate with you. This book isn't meant for those who consider themselves perfect. As the Bible reminds us, we are all sinners saved by grace, and we consistently fall short in the eyes of God.

This inspiring collection of books is designed for individuals who are ready to embrace personal empowerment. It is for those who have decided to say, "I will no longer be used or taken for granted. I will stand up for myself and for those who need help. I will refuse to accept abuse. From this point forward, I will take full control of my life. With God on my side, I will be victorious, and I will break free from anything holding me back. Finally, I will find peace."

I don't sugarcoat things. What value would this series have if I only shared what was comfortable instead of what truly helps you? My goal is to assist you in breaking free from the habits that hold you back, as well as the greed and selfishness that prevent us from acting out of love. I want to help you overcome internal desires that could jeopardize everything you have worked for. This collection is not intended to criticize; instead, it aims to empower you with practical solutions, resilient strategies for tough times, and enduring principles and wisdom that remain relevant today.

This will encourage you to reflect deeply on different aspects of your life and motivate you to make improvements if you choose to do so. If you take action, you can expect to see significant progress in various areas, such as your marriage, finances, family relationships, spiritual life, health, management, and wealth. These are often some of the most pressing concerns for people around the world.

Having faced numerous life challenges, including spiritual and marital struggles, as well as financial difficulties, I have come to understand the importance of self-management, focus, discipline, and self-determination. Since high school, I have recognized that I do not want to live paycheck to paycheck. I learned early on that relying on a single source of income can lead to stress, doubt, and fear. This understanding motivated me to launch several ventures in my early teens.

Throughout my journey, I experienced various ups and downs while trying to navigate life independently. Although I made many mistakes along the way, I recovered and committed myself to avoiding the same pitfalls in the future. For over twenty-five years, I have studied business, management, leadership, relationships, finance, investments, and the positive impact of having faith in God in my life.

These findings have not only helped me solve problems and create systems that work while I sleep, but they have also enabled me to achieve the life I've always dreamed of, bringing me happiness and joy. They have provided me with a strong spiritual foundation that keeps my family and me safe, enabling us to serve others and give back to society without expecting anything in return. Thanks to God's grace, we're currently experiencing the best time of our lives while helping others. However, I recognize that, despite how far I've come, there is still much more for me to accomplish.

I am deeply grateful for the opportunities I have had to work with, speak to, and learn from many experts across various fields and industries during my career and entrepreneurial journey. Many of these individuals have been exceptional mentors, counselors, advisors, and business leaders—men and women dedicated to helping others. They have inspired me to do the same.

As a result, I have had the opportunity to assist several families, students, and friends in overcoming various challenges and avoiding pitfalls related to life circumstances, manipulation, debt, and related issues. I hope you find the material I share in this collection helpful and motivating as you strive to access all the blessings that God has in store for you.

On behalf of my family and friends, thank you for choosing this book. I hope it brings blessings to you, your family, and your organization. While several effective strategies are presented, this collection primarily focuses on personal growth, transformation, self-management, spiritual growth, leadership, resilience, a positive mindset, patience, self-discipline, purpose, and more. Everyone should be the best captain of their lives, and every life should be lived to the fullest.

Many of us are constrained by forces intended to support us rather than hinder us, due to a lack of effective management and self-awareness. These natural forces can either propel us forward and help us build strong teams and relationships, or they can hold us back.

This collection of volumes will explore how individuals can harness various forces to their advantage. It will provide strategies, principles, and examples to unlock hidden potential and achieve new heights. Additionally, it will explain how these forces, along with our behaviors and emotions, can influence us and impact future generations.

I will examine preventive measures to protect yourself and others from human predators who seek to manipulate and exploit the vulnerable among us. Moreover, I will discuss how to become a knowledgeable individual who cannot be easily deceived or manipulated by others.

Some chapters in this collection will not only highlight the problems we face but also offer valuable insights on how to address them. These insights will include techniques, universal principles, and laws that govern our existence, helping you to see a new world of opportunities, wisdom, and power.

After reading this book, I hope you will become wiser and gain extensive knowledge that will help you make better decisions, see beyond the obvious, and apply insights in innovative ways. This collection aims to support anyone who wishes to improve their life and is willing to align their actions with God's will. By doing this, you can achieve significant accomplishments while also preparing for the return of our Lord and Savior, Jesus Christ.

Chapter 1

Life Is Not Neutral–Every Decision We Make Either Builds Or Erodes The World Around Us

One of God's first acts was to give life to everything. The earth was empty and formless, and God said, "Let there be light." From there, He went on to create all the other things we know, including humanity. Therefore, life itself must be significant in God's eyes. If it weren't, it wouldn't make sense for Jesus to die to save us from sin. This means that both your life and mine matter. We must cherish and take care of ourselves. Additionally, we should strive not just for today or tomorrow, but for the eternal life that God offers to everyone willing to accept it.

Nonetheless, eternal life is not easily attained; it largely depends on our actions and decisions. Therefore, life is a critical matter that should not be taken lightly or for granted. It is essential to value life and recognize its significance. Many people around the world feel that life is not worth living, but this perspective is not true. Life has so much to offer if we take the time to notice it. Despite all odds, life is filled with joy and countless treasures.

Some people believe that while life is important, it shouldn't be taken too seriously. They might ask, "Can't I live as I please as long as I do my job, care for my family, and pay my taxes?" While these questions are valid, life encompasses more than just a basic mindset and set of norms. A well-managed life yields far greater rewards than one simply focused on pleasure and indulgence.

We all have the right to live our lives as we choose. However, it's important to remember that we are not alone in this world. Even our simplest actions can have a significant impact on others. **What we do today can influence what happens tomorrow. Our choices shape the environment we live in, and the actions we take today will ultimately contribute to the world of tomorrow.**

Therefore, because we do not live on this planet alone, we must take life seriously and consider our actions–whether small or big–to create a better world for future generations if we genuinely care. It's essential to care about your family, including those around the world, as everything you do with, to, or for them will always impact the future. The key point is that our actions, thoughts, and decisions are all interconnected in some way. They often affect someone or something, whether directly or indirectly, intentionally or unintentionally. Therefore, we must be cautious and think before we act, because the consequences of our actions can endure and last for generations.

Every individual is precious, and therefore, every life is invaluable. While we may not always understand why someone might not appreciate life or feel it is worth taking seriously, we do know that numerous factors can negatively affect life and happiness. A person's thoughts and feelings about themselves can either empower them or lead them to have a diminished self-view. It's essential to recognize that you are always important–simply because you exist. You should feel unique and special every day, even when you don't feel good. Never compare yourself to others. You can look to others as guides or mentors, but remember that comparisons can be misleading and unhelpful.

Comparing your life or yourself to others can lead to unnecessary stress and make you think less of yourself or your situation. Two major threats to your happiness and peace are covetousness and envy. This is why the Bible states, "A sound heart is life to the body, but envy is rottenness to the bones" (Proverbs 14:30). Additionally, Exodus 20:17 strongly advises against coveting your neighbor's house, spouse, servants, livestock, or anything else they own. In other words, it's important to be satisfied with what you have. Doing so can bring peace and joy to your heart.

However, this doesn't mean you shouldn't have ambitions. Ambition is the drive to want more in life, but it should be focused on achieving what you work for rather than desiring someone else's property. Therefore, if you aspire to obtain something, pursue that goal in ways that do not compromise your integrity or morals.

Let's take a look at the story of Luna and Mr. Hallman. Every morning, Luna walked past Mr. Hallman's house on Willgrove Street. His garden, bursting with roses, sunflowers, and delicate bluebells that resembled tiny bells of the sky, always caught her eye. Neighbors often stopped to admire his beautiful garden. As Luna gazed at the flowers, she found herself wishing her own yard could look even half as lovely.

One afternoon, after a long day, she paused at the edge of Mr. Hallman's fence, thinking, "Why can't my garden look like this? Why does he have all this beauty?" A tightness formed in her chest—envy.

Just then, Mr. Hallman stepped outside with a watering can. "Good evening, Luna!" he said warmly. "Admiring the roses?"

She forced a smile and replied, "They're beautiful. I wish my garden looked like that."

He chuckled and said, "Well, these old hands have spent years tending to them - countless early mornings and a few failures, too."

Luna blinked. She had never considered the work behind the beauty—only the result.

As she arrived home, she looked at her own patch of earth differently. It wasn't much—just some struggling daisies and a few stubborn weeds—but she realized it was hers. With a bit of care and attention, she could shape it.

The next morning, instead of looking at Mr. Hallman's blossoms with longing, she grabbed her gloves and knelt in her own yard. She pulled weeds, loosened the soil, and planted new seeds. The process demanded slow, patient work. Sometimes it was frustrating; other times, it was quietly joyful.

Weeks passed, and her garden grew—small, imperfect, and alive. One morning, she stood up, brushed dirt from her knees, and smiled. Not because it looked like Mr. Hallman's garden, but because it didn't. It looked like hers—colorful and beautiful.

When Mr. Hallman walked by and admired her progress, she no longer felt envy; instead, she felt gratitude. She had stopped wishing for someone else's blessings and started tending her own garden. In doing so, she discovered something better than beauty: peace.

Let's take a closer look at the story of two friends, Jennifer and Sara.

Jennifer and Sara graduated from college around the same time, filled with hope and expectations for what life would bring. However, as the years passed, their paths began to diverge significantly. Sara's life unfolded effortlessly. She married a kind and successful man, built a loving family with two children, and settled into a beautiful home in a comfortable, affluent neighborhood. In contrast, Jennifer struggled; life did not go as she had planned, and for a while, the two friends lost touch.

Years later, Sara reached out and invited Jennifer to reconnect. When Jennifer arrived at Sara's home, her heart sank. The house was stunning, the family was joyful, and their life appeared polished in ways that Jennifer's own life was not. As Sara gave her a tour, Jennifer smiled politely, but inside, she felt a quiet ache. Comparison crept in, and she began to wonder why her life had taken such a different path. For a brief moment, envy whispered that Sara had everything she lacked.

Once they were sitting together, the two women talked and laughed. Sara spoke gratefully about meeting her husband and how fortunate she felt. When it was Jennifer's turn to share, her story was heavier. "The man I thought would be my husband left me with two children and a pile of bills," she admitted. Her words were honest, and they carried the weight of her pain.

As the conversation continued, something shifted within Jennifer. Instead of letting envy harden her heart, she paused to reflect. She realized that coveting Sara's life would only rob her of peace. Looking at her friend, she chose a different response. With sincerity, she said, "I'm happy we met again. You motivate me." Then she asked, "How did you and Ben build all of this?" Smiling gently, she added, "If you can do it, maybe I can too."

When Jennifer left that day, she felt mixed emotions, but one thing was clear: she would no longer measure her worth against Sara's success. Rather than envying what she did not have, she chose to believe in what was still possible. Reconnecting with Sara became a turning point for her, not a source of bitterness, but a catalyst for growth.

At that time, Jennifer was still renting, driving an old car, and struggling to make ends meet. Yet her heart was lighter. She found peace by focusing on her own journey instead of longing for someone else's life. She returned to school, earned her master's degree in a field similar to Sara's, and eventually started a home-based business. She worked hard, remained patient, and trusted the process.

Ten years later, Jennifer's life looked very different. Although she was still single, she was earning more than Sara and her husband combined. She had built a life rooted in stability, fulfillment, and self-respect. When Jennifer invited Sara to her housewarming party, the joy was genuine. With a warm smile, Jennifer said, "I told you I could do it. I told you I'd get there." They shared a laugh as Jennifer gave her friend a tour of her new home.

Jennifer's success was not born from envy, jealousy, or coveting. Instead, it grew from choosing peace over comparison and love over resentment. She learned that it's perfectly fine to want success—but it must be pursued in the right way. True friends inspire rather than compete and encourage rather than provoke jealousy.

Jennifer never tried to become Sara. Instead, she allowed Sara's life to remind her of what was possible. By letting go of envy, Jennifer found her own path—and along that path, she discovered both success and peace.

How can you navigate the challenges that threaten your well-being? What strategies can help you maintain a positive outlook on life, especially during stressful and chaotic times? How can you overcome feelings of envy towards others, particularly when it seems like their lives are better than yours?

Start by practicing gratitude for each new day. Every day alive is filled with possibilities—an opportunity to explore new approaches until you discover what works for you. When you wake up, take a moment to pray and express your thanks for life. Acknowledge your weaknesses and your need for support. Be open to asking for help, seeking it out, and accepting the assistance that comes your way, no matter how small it may seem.

I remember a time when I needed money for gas and found some on the street. After counting it, I realized it was only two dollars. I felt frustrated and exclaimed, "Aren't You God Almighty? Don't You own thousands of cattle on the hills? Don't You see my needs? And You only give me two lousy dollars? Are You serious, God? Couldn't You do better?"

Then, I understood that God was not just teaching me the value of money but also providing me with enough to purchase the gas I needed to get home. I should have been grateful and thanked Him in that moment.

So, give thanks whenever help comes your way, whether it's small or big. Always try to see the bright side of things. Dream big and collaborate with others to achieve those dreams. Be patient as you work towards your goals, and celebrate every blessing. Avoid feelings of envy, jealousy, and competition. Remember, it's your life and your goals—you don't need to compete with anyone else. Everyone has their own path. If you remain patient and work each day diligently toward your objectives, you will eventually reach them. The feeling of achieving something you work for is marvelous, and the more you feel that life is worth living.

If you do not take control of your life, it will take control of you. Think about it! While we all share similarities in our bodies and organs, each person is uniquely designed with their own blueprint. The art of management is not only inherent in our DNA but also in the laws that govern our bodies and minds.

Every moment you spend alive is a blessing, regardless of how you live. Strive to do your best each day. Keep moving forward, even when times are tough, and you feel uncertain about your next steps. Now, let's explore deeper lessons that can help you strengthen your resilience, tackle greater challenges, and empower others to do the same.

Key Takeaways

- Value your life and the lives of others.
- When facing challenges, always remember that someone else is enduring something even more difficult than you are. That person perseveres through their pain, and so can you.
- Collaborate with others and appreciate every ounce of help you receive.
- Cultivate patience daily, as the journey to true success is often long.
- Enjoy life whenever possible, but continue to move forward despite the challenges you face.
- Do not covet, envy, compete, or compare yourself with anyone.
- You are running your own race, guided by your time, strength, and mindset.

Chapter 2

Do Not Put All Your Problems In One Basket

A significant mistake many people make when facing life's challenges is categorizing all issues under a single label: "life." While we often encounter similar challenges, it's crucial to recognize that they require different approaches if we want to address them effectively. It would be unwise to think that we can resolve every problem in the same way or with the same strategy. For example, dealing with a fever demands a different approach than managing a demanding boss or navigating a troubled marriage. Similarly, you wouldn't use the same methods to tackle financial issues.

Since not all challenges are the same, we cannot treat them as if they are. Thus, it's essential to develop distinct action plans or response strategies for the various difficulties we encounter. Remember, the more prepared you are each day, the better your chances of success. If you consistently apply the principles discussed in this book, you will ultimately reap the rewards of living a well-managed and balanced life, supported by both automatic and intentional systems.

Life and time are incredibly precious. Do not waste them; instead, make the most of the time and life you have right now. Strive to improve yourself daily so that you can be a more effective helper for others. Throughout these chapters, I aim to help you gain perspective on your life, encourage you to think outside the box, and empower you to stand up for yourself. Everything in your life and surroundings can work to your benefit if you learn how to set those elements in motion to serve you.

Do not approach life with ambiguity. Treat every day like a war. Not a war against people, but mainly against our bad habits, pride, greed, insecurity, and the problems that come to us unexpectedly.

We often hesitate to work on ourselves and instead blame others for the issues we may actually be responsible for. For instance, we neglect to turn off the lights when they are not in use, and then complain about high electric bills. Sometimes, we speak without thinking, and then we can't take back our words or undo the damage caused. As human beings, we face many setbacks.

By categorizing our problems, we can create specific action plans that address each issue more effectively. It's important not to treat every event or situation as if they are the same. Just as different types of fruit are organized in a market—such as oranges in one section and bananas in another—we must identify potential events or problems that may come to our door and categorize them accordingly. By doing so, we can plan for each issue more efficiently and effectively. Recognizing these challenges in advance is crucial for successful planning.

Take Christopher, for example. He has a beautiful family of four, but also carries thousands of dollars in debt and student loans. Although he has a good job, he often arrives late, grumpy, and looking disheveled. He constantly complains and is usually the first to leave work each day. When he goes home, he continues the same pattern: complaining and failing to support his wife as he should. Instead, he spends his time drinking, watching football, and repeating the same cycle. His employer and family have given him several chances to change his habits, but he has never made an effort to do so. Eventually, his boss grew tired of his attitude and fired him. When he returned home that day, he found no one there; his wife and children had left.

Peter, who lives across the street, had a similar experience to Christopher, but he approached his problems differently when his boss first addressed him. Peter recognized that he needed to provide for his family, so he understood that not taking his job seriously was a significant issue he had to confront. His marriage was also struggling, and he knew he needed to take action regarding that as well. Additionally, he acknowledged that he had an anger management problem that required attention.

Unlike many people, Peter didn't feel sorry for himself and call it "Life!" He didn't treat every problem as if they were the same and then move on. Instead, after some deep self-reflection, Peter created a simple plan for each situation. He realized he had to take action. He enrolled in a support group to help him address his drinking and anger issues. He developed strategies and techniques to improve his coping skills and communication during stressful or frustrating moments.

He incorporated a twenty-minute exercise routine and five minutes of meditation into his daily schedule. While this may seem minimal, both practices significantly benefited him. The exercise helped reduce his stress, while the meditation helped manage his anger.

To improve his work performance, Peter set a specific time to stop all activities by 10:00 p.m. and go to bed, ensuring he wouldn't have difficulty getting up in the morning. He also scheduled a specific time to leave the house, allowing him to arrive at least fifteen minutes early. After work, he dedicated time to enhance his marriage by reading books and attending workshops with his wife, sometimes going alone.

Two years later, his life had transformed completely. He had become one of the most admired employees at work, and his relationships with his wife and children had never been better. Peter remained consistent in his progress and never reverted to his previous state. Now, he is helping others recover from similar situations.

Key Takeaways

- Identify all of your problems or issues, and write them down.
- Analyze each problem and create a specific plan to address each one separately.
- Actively follow up on your plans. Work on each plan for at least 30 days.
- After the first 30 days, review each plan and assess your progress.
- Make adjustments as necessary.
- Once you have an effective routine or plan, continue it for 60 to 90 days.
- Keep practicing it until it becomes automatic or a part of your daily life.
- Stay focused on yourself and the goals you want to achieve.
- Remind yourself why you don't want to fall victim to procrastination, carelessness, and laziness.

Chapter 3

Work On Your Puzzle. Everyone Has One

Life is real, and so are you. The circumstances that happen in your life are also factual. Therefore, it's important to approach life with purpose, intention, and strategies that distinguish you from others. Aim to go through each day with well-thought-out actions and plans. No day should pass without making progress toward a goal—whether it's short-term or long-term—related to yourself, your family, or your community.

Human life is like a large puzzle, where all the pieces must come together to reveal the complete picture. The more effort you dedicate to finding and fitting the right pieces, the sooner you'll see the bigger picture or the overarching plan for your life. By continually working on yourself, even in small daily increments, you'll improve, clarify your vision, and move closer to achieving your goals and dreams. This is why every single day of your life matters.

Many times, we become discouraged and stop working on ourselves and pursuing our dreams when things don't go our way. However, despite the challenges, there are many aspects of our journey or puzzle we can focus on to regain our strength and energy before tackling the most difficult parts. It's important to remember that most people fail simply because they either stop trying or try to skip the essential processes we must go through before we can finally reap the harvest.

We often want to achieve the big picture without first assembling the smaller pieces. If we overlook these steps, we risk not becoming the person we are meant to be or fully maturing. Sometimes, in the face of life's difficulties, we need to push through the tough moments and learn from them to become the best version of ourselves. The key is to never give up or stop working on ourselves and our dreams, despite setbacks.

Problems and challenges are an inevitable part of life. While we can prevent certain issues or drama from arising, there are circumstances we cannot avoid. Therefore, the best approach is to equip ourselves with the right techniques, strategies, and mindset to overcome the challenges we encounter, regardless of our background, economic status, education, or profession.

It is unnecessary to list all the potential challenges and difficulties we may face, as they can take various forms, differ in magnitude, and occur at different times for each individual. The reality is that we all encounter obstacles and hardships in life. Thus, it is crucial to recognize the things we cannot control and understand their impact on ourselves, our families, and our goals and dreams.

Remember, if we do not take life seriously, we automatically forfeit our goals and dreams, and in some cases, we also make it difficult for those around us to fulfill theirs.

So, how do you stay motivated despite the setbacks and challenges you face? How do you keep pushing through life even when you feel exhausted or lack the strength and courage? First, remind yourself that you are not here by accident. Believe that you were sent to Earth for a specific purpose. Even if you don't know what that purpose is yet, tell yourself that you will discover it soon, or that it will be revealed to you in due time. Be patient with yourself and continue moving forward in the meantime.

If you're feeling overwhelmed, it doesn't mean you should rush back to the task or event that caused it, unless it's necessary. If the situation can wait, take a moment to step away. Try taking a break and going for a walk, or talking to a friend for a few minutes. If you prefer, you can visit your local store to pick up any items you need. While you're doing these simple activities, be open to connecting with others if you can. Instead of using self-checkout, engage with a real person by chatting with the cashier or anyone else you meet while shopping. You could ask the cashier, "How are you doing? How was your day?" These small interactions can help reset your mood and enhance your overall workday experience.

The human mind was never designed to remain alone for long periods or to be glued to a screen without taking breaks. We were created for meaningful interactions with real people, and our system craves this connection. We often seek it out to feel valued, appreciated, and heard. This is part of our nature; when pursued correctly and for the right reasons, these interactions benefit both our body and mind.

If you prefer a more independent approach, consider taking a moment for self-care, such as showering, getting your nails done, or enjoying a massage. Even stepping outside your porch or front door to take a deep breath of fresh air can help remind you why you should keep going and not give up.

When life feels heavy and challenges seem overwhelming, take a moment to pause and speak words of strength to yourself. Remind yourself that you are capable, resilient, and equipped to keep moving forward. Sometimes, a few encouraging words are all it takes to shift your mindset and renew your energy. Positive self-talk is a powerful tool; it can support you during difficult moments, lift you when you're feeling low, and guide you toward wiser, more hopeful choices. When practiced with intention, positive self-talk becomes a source of support, confidence, and inner peace. You can even train your self-talk to defend you when you're feeling down or when you want to avoid making choices you might regret later.

For instance, when your mind says, "You cannot do something," remind yourself: "I can do it. I'm just feeling frustrated right now, and that's okay."

If it tells you, "You don't have what it takes," respond with, "I do have what it takes. I just need a moment, and I will figure it out eventually."

When it says, "You will never get it right," counter with, "That's not true. I may not be an expert in this area, but I am capable of learning and finding a solution."

If it claims, "You will always be the same," say, "That's false. I may not be fully developed or mature yet, but I will grow."

Lastly, remind yourself: "My past does not define me. I will change, I will adapt, and I will become better and greater."

The more you train that cognitive process to speak more positively than negatively, the better your self-talk can support you during some of the most challenging times of your life.

The key to these exercises is to take a moment to reflect at the end of each day. Ask yourself, "What helped me return to my normal state or get back on track when I was feeling down today?" Take note of your responses or record them. The next time you encounter a setback, you may discover new insights that can help you recover more quickly. Write down these activities and observations. Over time, you'll compile a strong list of effective reactions, strategies, and coping techniques that will assist you in escaping setbacks and navigating difficult moments more effectively.

Consider Richard, for example. He is a highly motivated individual, always driven to accomplish something. People describe him as a builder, a self-starter, and a go-getter–the kind of person who navigates life fearlessly. Public speaking and hosting shows have never intimidated him. He has a charming, motivating presence and is kind and loving. With ambitious goals and aspirations, Richard's future looks exceptionally bright.

However, one day, Richard found himself struggling with depression. It all began when he started feeling unmotivated. He spent more time lying in bed, engulfed in sadness, and avoided going out. Fear and self-doubt consumed him throughout the day. This shift began after he experienced a devastating incident or loss. Richard had no clue what was happening to him, unsure of why he felt so strange, scared, and unmotivated. He recognized that he was no longer the person he used to be. Although he couldn't figure out the cause of his feelings, he knew he had to do something.

Richard started to confront the new version of himself that he didn't like. He began to monitor his daily routine and question his actions. Whenever he felt strange or uninterested in something, he didn't just acknowledge those feelings; he investigated their causes. Then, he took significant steps to change his responses, no matter how painful the process felt.

In the midst of his depression, a friend invited Richard to speak at an event. Rather than declining the invitation, Richard accepted it, even though he was still struggling with symptoms. He understood that the only way to recover was to confront every challenge head-on, despite his mind instinctively urging him to run away, retreat, and reject any opportunities that arose. Instead of saying no, he chose to say yes whenever someone asked for his help. His intention was not to ignore his problems but to use these opportunities as motivation to get out of bed, avoid isolation, and eliminate excuses for not participating. Ultimately, the more he pushed himself to stay active, the quicker he found his way to recovery.

Even though Richard was feeling better and able to return to his everyday life, the signs of depression occasionally returned. Determined not to let depression affect him again, he started to reflect on how he had ended up in that situation. He questioned what he had done wrong and where he had missed the mark. To confront these challenges, he began writing down his patterns and developing a specific plan to address the moments or events that triggered his depression. Whenever he felt sad, worthless, or agitated, he listened to motivational audiobooks and uplifting songs that lifted his spirits.

When Richard feels tempted to avoid a responsibility or activity, he makes a conscious effort to follow through. He is determined not to let depression control him again. To tackle this challenge, he documented every symptom he experienced during his bouts of depression and created a specific plan to address each one.

When he feels fatigued or sleepy, he chooses to volunteer or take his kids to the movies or another fun outing. If he feels overwhelmed, he either spends time in prayer or watches one of his favorite movies, allowing himself to enjoy it without guilt. Richard actively confronts each symptom, fighting back against his depression until it no longer has power over him.

Similarly, it's important to recognize what you are fighting against or recovering from. Then, develop specific techniques to combat these challenges. Like Richard, you can use various methods to protect yourself not only from depression but also from other forms of anxiety. Embrace a vibrant lifestyle by prioritizing sleep, adopting a balanced diet (with minimal or no sugar), and committing to regular exercise. Start with just 10 minutes of activity each day, gradually increasing to 30 minutes, and eventually 40, until you find what works best for you. Remember, the goal isn't to be perfect; it's about making consistent, positive changes. Consistency is what truly matters.

Other effective techniques for reducing stress and depression include building strong social connections and engaging in enjoyable or creative activities. If you haven't done so already, consider creating a bucket list that includes items or activities requiring only your time.

Explore the world or nearby cities by hiking or biking. Spend time in nature, visit different parks, go camping, or attend free local events. You can invite someone you trust to join you, or you can go solo if you prefer. Remember, you don't always need to be the center of attention; it's important to learn to work independently. The ultimate goal is to become resilient enough that nothing can hold you back or keep you down.

Managing stress can be difficult, but staying engaged with life can greatly enhance your health and peace of mind. It's essential to avoid living with feelings of anger or resentment. Make an effort to resolve conflicts, even with those who have wronged you. Reach out to friends and extended family when possible. When these strategies are practiced in a balanced way and at a reasonable pace, they can lead to significant improvements, helping you experience less tension, stress, illness, and chaos. This approach can also assist you in reconnecting and mending relationships that you once thought were beyond repair.

Remember, as long as you live, life will continue to throw you many curveballs. Some you will successfully dodge, while others may hit you. Regardless of what happens, you cannot give up. Understanding that giving up isn't an option will allow you to prepare for the days ahead. In the next chapter, we will explore more potential challenges that can bring us down, divert us from our dreams, or make life exceedingly difficult. By understanding these challenges, you'll be better equipped for the journey ahead and will gain valuable knowledge on how to recover more quickly than expected.

Key Takeaway

- Never let anything hold you down.
- Acknowledge the challenges you're facing.
- Train your self-talk to support you rather than undermine you.
- Observe and record what helps you when you're feeling down, sad, or unmotivated.
- Fight back against every setback or obstacle until you succeed.
- Reflect on yourself, your problems, and progress every day; these reflections should motivate you to wake up and fight each day.
- Stay focused on your goals until you complete the entire picture or until your dreams become a reality.

Chapter 4

The Battlefields No One Can Avoid. But We Can Prepare For Them

Life itself can feel like a battlefield. The areas where the enemy's influence is felt can be vast and may affect many aspects of your life, such as a workplace you dislike or a home that fails to provide the peace you seek. This negative influence might extend to your church or school as well. Sometimes, you may even discover that you are your own worst enemy. Therefore, being prepared and aware of the enemy's terrain is crucial. This understanding can be invaluable; it can reveal how unprepared you genuinely are and indicate the specific tools and strategies you need before entering or engaging in any conflict or battle.

If you are aware that your enemy has a weapon capable of destroying you with invisible forces, you would naturally want to learn more about it. Simply understanding this weapon of mass destruction is not enough; you would also need to know what strategies or resources you have to defend against it. Entering a war or conflict with such an adversary without sufficient knowledge, preparation, or tactics would be unwise.

Let's examine this topic more closely. Each person has an inner battlefield that needs to be managed. It is crucial to take complete control of it because, if you don't, the devil can and will use it against you. This is why the Bible states, "And if your right hand causes you to sin, cut it off and cast it from you; for it is more profitable for you that one of your members perish than for your whole body to be cast into hell." To emphasize the seriousness of this warning, Jesus reiterated it in another way: "If your right eye causes you to sin, pluck it out and cast it from you; for it is more profitable for you that one of your members perish than for your whole body to be cast into hell" (Matthew 5:29-32). These statements may sound harsh, but they were not intended to judge us; rather, they serve as a warning to protect us from the dangers that lie within ourselves. **Specific behaviors, cravings, or desires can become the battleground we need to confront before we can achieve true freedom.**

Consider Robert, for example. He suffers from type 2 diabetes, and his physician advised him to avoid sugar. The doctor clearly explained how sugar could worsen his condition and put his health at risk. After his first major surgery, Robert, who had a strong love for sugar, resolved to abstain from it. Whenever he craved sugar, he chose to drink water instead. By turning his craving into a positive habit, he ultimately saved his own life.

If he had followed the doctor's advice earlier, he could have prevented many of the issues he faced. However, he continued his sugary habits until he confronted the fear of death in the operating room. Since that experience, he has avoided all substances and foods containing glucose. Though it was challenging, he committed to adopting a healthier lifestyle.

We always have the option to take control of any battlefield that threatens us if we make the choice to do so. As Jesus advised, we must not allow anything within us to become our adversary or a weapon in the devil's hands, especially when we possess the power to control our impulses, resist temptations, and manage our deepest desires.

Additionally, life's unforeseen circumstances can often feel like enemies. The list of unavoidable events throughout our lives can be quite long. For example, we cannot prevent the following events from occurring or knocking us to our knees: the loss of loved ones, illness, or the poor and selfish decisions of others. There will be times when you feel down, sad, and unmotivated to carry on. Everything may seem off, and despite your best efforts, nothing appears to be working. These moments are real, and when they arise, it's essential to find ways to motivate yourself so that you don't isolate yourself from the world and the people around you.

During these tough times, it's important to give yourself a pep talk, reminding yourself that you are valuable to the world, regardless of what others may say. You have the power to change your direction and keep moving forward in life. Don't allow yourself, or anyone else, to trap you in a cycle of negativity. As long as you're alive, you matter. You are important, and you can make a positive difference in your own life and in the lives of others.

However, some events in life are inevitable; no one can escape them. Everyone must eventually confront these experiences. Losing a loved one can have a profound impact not only on you but also on your family and community, especially if the person played a significant role in that community. This includes the loss of a husband who was the primary support for his wife and children or the loss of an only child. Sudden illnesses, like a stroke or cancer, can also take a loved one unexpectedly. These events can occur at any time without warning and have the power to deeply affect a person both emotionally and mentally.

In some cases, it may take days for a person to recover or overcome the situation. Although this is unlikely to occur due to the brokenness of human nature, only God can prevent a person from facing these events entirely. Throughout history, we've seen instances where God engaged with specific individuals, making extraordinary exceptions for them because of their personal relationship with Him. Enoch and Elijah are among those who found favor before God to such a degree that God sent a host of angels to take these individuals and spare them from experiencing death or terrible illnesses that would otherwise impact their lives just like everyone else. Nonetheless, we do not know whether these men had not faced or encountered some of these events before their departure or journey with God. Unfortunately, most of us will, in some way, experience some of these events.

So, why do we discuss death and illness in a book about self-management and personal growth? Too often, managers, professionals, and leaders overlook these events and their potential impact on the individuals they lead. Ignoring the effects of such experiences can lead us to act contrary to God's principles and laws.

For example, I witnessed a friend named Eric endure some incredibly tough times for about six years. He described that period as the most terrible and difficult of his life. During those years, compounded by the COVID-19 pandemic, he faced significant financial and emotional challenges. His business filed for bankruptcy, his mother was dying, he lost his dog, and his marriage was in turmoil. After his mother passed away, Eric discovered that his wife was having an affair. It felt as if he couldn't catch a break, with problems coming one after another. At one point, he wondered if God had forgotten about him.

The problems, or so-called surprising events, that we discussed earlier kept occurring one after another. Despite this, Eric remained in a leadership position that required his presence and attention. Even with his world turned upside down and under immense stress, he still had to go to work and act as if everything was fine. However, deep down, he felt like he was not entirely himself. At times, he could be mean; on other days, he was bitter, consumed by anger and resentment. He found himself reluctant to talk to anyone and felt as if his life was over. "Going to work or home was no longer enjoyable," he said. "I began to isolate myself and eventually fell into a deep depression without even realizing it," Eric admitted. Fortunately, God saved him. "When I finally came to my senses, I recognized how powerful the effects of these unforeseen life events can be on a person when they are not addressed immediately and properly," he reported.

Why is it important to address these situations promptly? Acting quickly does not mean rushing through the grieving process; rather, it means starting to prepare as soon as you know a loved one is nearing the end of their life. It is crucial to prepare yourself both emotionally and financially before facing the inevitable.

Additionally, it is vital to allow yourself the necessary time to navigate through grief, knowing that your responsibilities are taken care of and your company is in capable hands. Even if you continue working, prioritizing your emotional well-being and addressing your feelings during this challenging time should be a top priority.

Make sure to set aside time to engage with the grieving process. Reflect, pray, and seek strength and direction. Avoid ignoring the situation or pretending that everything is fine. Failing to address these emotions can have lasting effects that may impact you in ways you're not even aware of. Remember, you are human; it is essential to process your emotions properly so you can move forward in life effectively.

Do you remember Joseph from the Bible? He is the same Joseph who was sold into slavery by his own brothers and later became second-in-command after Pharaoh. As one of Egypt's leaders, Joseph serves as a prominent example to many, not only for his exceptional leadership and management skills but also for his humility and compassion.

After the death of his father, Israel—also known as Jacob—Joseph mourned for approximately forty days. The entire community mourned for seventy days, as recorded in Genesis 50:1-5. In addition to this, Joseph observed another seven days of mourning, which were deeply personal for him, as he was his father's beloved son.

Joseph also requested permission from Pharaoh to go to Canaan to bury his father, as he had promised. This narrative highlights the importance for leaders to acknowledge and address the physical, emotional, mental, and spiritual forces that can impact them just like anyone else.

Genesis 35:16-20 tells us that Jacob also took time to grieve the loss of his wife, Rachel. As leaders, it is vital for us to manage our own emotions and actions, because we are responsible for serving others who may not have the strength to navigate life's challenges as we do. Therefore, it is essential to understand each moment in our lives and strategically prioritize our time to address our problems effectively, without disrupting our work or the lives of those who depend on us.

While we cannot avoid difficult experiences, they are an inevitable part of life. Their effects will continue to influence us and shape our futures. However, we should not allow these events to hinder our progress or advancement in life. God allows certain events to occur for a reason. Although these experiences may be painful, we must take them seriously and respond appropriately.

In many cases, the challenges we encounter serve as lessons that God allows us to experience in order to strengthen and develop our character. Without these experiences, many of us might not have become the genuine and authentic individuals we are today. Although these events can feel overwhelming and difficult, they provide us with valuable knowledge, endurance, perseverance, and even hope. Ultimately, they equip us with insights and experiences that transform us and prepare us for future challenges. After all, God promises that He works all things for good and will never leave us nor forsake us, no matter what we face.

Take Andrew, for example. He grew up in one of the toughest neighborhoods in Detroit, where his family struggled to make ends meet. Living in a two-bedroom apartment with his eight siblings, they barely had enough food to eat. Despite their circumstances, his parents instilled in them the belief that they had no reason to engage in illegal activities. Andrew watched many of his friends lead better lives, but he also witnessed the tragic consequences of poor choices, attending the funerals of close friends who sought wealth through the fastest and easiest means available.

His parents taught him to fight for what is good and right, regardless of the challenges they faced. Some days, there was not enough food for everyone, so the younger siblings had to eat first, leaving Andrew with whatever was left—sometimes just barely enough to sustain him for the day. During these difficult times, his parents often reminded them of the saying, "Man shall not live by bread alone," which became a common phrase in their household. For Andrew, this phrase meant more than mere survival; it inspired him to resist temptations, build resilience, and prioritize the well-being of others.

Twenty years later, Andrew started his first business with a few friends, hoping for a better life. However, within the first two years, the company collapsed. His friends took advantage of him and left him with more debt than he could handle. After recovering from that setback, he launched another business. This time, he had a family to care for, so things needed to work out. Andrew could not afford to lose any money, but he didn't let fear hold him back. He moved forward with his business, this time armed with more planning, preparation, and strategy. Despite his dedication, which included many late nights and early mornings, his company went bankrupt after five years. Andrew felt heartbroken and disappointed.

After that experience, he decided to take a break and return to work to provide for his family. However, a couple of years later, he found that he could not find peace. The idea of owning his own business kept haunting him. Determined, he began saving aggressively. He remembered the quotes his parents had taught him during tough times. With this motivation, Andrew started managing every aspect of his expenses. He reviewed old records from his failed businesses and studied what went wrong, identifying where he could have pivoted to avoid failure.

As part of his plan, he cut his personal expenses by 70 percent to save even more. He recalled the saying, "Man shall not live by bread alone," which reminded him of how he once survived with very little. Thus, in his current life, as long as he had the basic necessities and his family was taken care of, he felt content. He realized that he didn't need a fancy watch or expensive suits; rather, he didn't need anything that would become a liability or lose value. Therefore, Andrew committed to using every failure as a learning opportunity to sharpen his leadership skills and character, ultimately gaining knowledge that perhaps even formal education could not provide.

Despite his growing confidence to launch a new venture, Andrew decided not to do so immediately. Instead, he continued working, earned a higher salary, saved more, and developed his management skills. A few years later, he finally launched the same business idea he had considered before. Many people thought he was making a mistake. However, Andrew not only had in-depth knowledge of the business and industry, but he was also aware of potential threats that could jeopardize the company. This time, he didn't quit his job abruptly. Instead, he gradually built the company until it was clear that it could generate three times his current salary.

God allows us to experience challenging times to help us mature and develop our character and wisdom. There is always an opportunity for personal growth. Often, true growth can only happen by learning new things, facing bigger challenges, making mistakes, and taking risks. It is our responsibility to push ourselves to do more, acquire new knowledge and skills, and improve both ourselves and our surroundings. Therefore, we must embrace life with all its challenges and joys.

In this context, the decisions of others that involve us can lead to uncomfortable moments and difficult situations. Before we proceed to the other sections of this book, I want to share insights I believe were inspired by God regarding the events and circumstances that can impact us as leaders. It would be a disservice not to elaborate on this topic, as these insights may help you navigate these challenges when they arise.

Others will inevitably wrong you, whether intentionally or unintentionally. In other words, there may come a day when you find yourself a victim of someone else's actions. Since we are the only ones who truly know our own thoughts—aside from God—it is impossible to understand what others genuinely think about us or the situations that involve us based on their decisions. Sometimes, it may be easy to read and predict a person's future actions based on their morals, past behavior, ethics, and character. However, it can be even more heartbreaking when those we least expect to hurt us turn out to be the ones who break our hearts.

Imagine a team leader named Victoria who is responsible for guiding her group through an important project. One day, she discovers that a major deadline was missed due to a misunderstanding among the team members. This delay impacts the entire team, leaving her feeling frustrated and disheartened.

In many cases, leaders may react emotionally by raising their voices, publicly blaming individuals, or making hasty decisions out of anger. Such reactions can exacerbate the situation, damaging trust and lowering morale. Instead of fostering a collaborative environment, these responses may make team members feel defensive rather than focused on finding a solution.

Nevertheless, Victoria takes the time to manage her emotions before responding to the team. She calmly gathers everyone together, listens to each person's perspective, and identifies where communication broke down. Instead of assigning blame, she focuses on finding solutions by adjusting the timeline, clarifying roles, and creating a better communication plan. Her composed approach helps the team regain focus, stay motivated, and work together to meet the new deadline.

This example illustrates that leaders who effectively manage their emotions can:

- Make fair and thoughtful decisions
- Maintain trust and respect within their teams
- Turn problems into opportunities for growth
- Create a positive and productive work environment

Leaders who manage their emotions well are more likely to make decisions that benefit both their team and the organization in the long run.

Therefore, as leaders, we cannot always control or prevent negative occurrences; thus, we must learn to adapt quickly while ensuring we do not harm others in the process. This is why the Bible advises us to be wise as serpents yet harmless as doves. One of the toughest challenges leaders face is dealing with betrayal or ethical failures from trusted team members. When someone we rely on breaks our trust–through dishonesty, misuse of authority, or pursuing personal agendas–it can significantly damage morale, credibility, and unity within the team. The Bible states, "The Lord detests lying lips, but He delights in people who are trustworthy." – Proverbs 12:22.

Let's explore how Roberto applied this biblical principle during a challenging moment in his career. As a school principal, he discovered that a longtime trusted assistant had been manipulating school data to make program outcomes appear more successful than they were. Because this assistant was highly respected and trusted by the entire staff, Roberto understood that confronting the issue could lead to division and backlash.

Rather than reacting with anger or seeking to expose his colleague publicly, Roberto first met privately with the assistant to discuss the issue honestly and respectfully. His goal was correction, not humiliation.

The assistant acknowledged his mistake and took responsibility for it. In response, Roberto established clear accountability measures, corrected the data transparently, and mandated ethical training for the leadership team. While the assistant faced appropriate consequences, Roberto chose to focus on repentance, learning, and rebuilding trust instead of seeking revenge, despite feeling deeply upset.

By grounding his response in biblical principles–such as truthfulness, private correction, and restoration–Roberto maintained his integrity, demonstrated ethical courage, and reinforced a culture of honesty. As a result, trust within the organization was ultimately strengthened, and his credibility increased through the balance of fairness and compassion.

In many situations, the principles outlined in the Bible remain relevant today. These lessons remind leaders that authority should be exercised with wisdom and grace. When addressing betrayal, it is important to do so directly yet with the intention of restoring relationships rather than causing harm. This approach helps leaders navigate one of the most painful challenges in modern leadership while maintaining moral clarity and promoting organizational health.

This principle is crucial not only in interactions with others but also in managing our own emotions as we confront life's difficulties. Leaders should cultivate a resilient mindset that prioritizes God, peace, and love. Even when someone wrongs you, it is essential to resist the desire for revenge. Instead, present the situation to God and allow Him to handle it. Acting in this manner demonstrates your dependence on God to seek justice on your behalf and reflects your trust in Him to fight your battles.

Most importantly, God's peace will be with you, allowing your heart to remain at ease even when you face the most challenging situations. When God sees that you trust Him, He will go above and beyond to protect and fight for you. You will overcome whatever you are going through, even when the struggle is caused by the actions of others. This is why David declared, "Though I walk through the valley of the shadow of death, I will fear no evil; for You are with me" (Psalm 23:4). David recognized that God was beside him, even in his most difficult circumstances. Because of this understanding, David learned to remain calm and to communicate with God during times of trouble throughout his life.

As leaders, we must learn to do the same. There are some situations in life from which only God can help you recover. If you fail to acknowledge this and attempt to solve these problems on your own, you may end up creating a deeper struggle for yourself rather than finding a resolution.

While there are issues we can control and problems we can solve, as leaders, we must also accept that some challenges are beyond our capacity to fix. These situations often require divine intervention. Great leaders understand their limits; they recognize when they cannot resolve a problem on their own and when they need guidance that comes from God's wisdom and understanding. They are not afraid to seek God's help in making and executing sound decisions.

Unfortunately, many leaders today do not believe in God and fail to seek His guidance during difficult times. Instead, they rely on their own knowledge and earthly connections rather than on God's divine wisdom and power. They often forget the words of God: "My thoughts are not your thoughts, neither are your ways My ways" (Isaiah 55:8-9). They also overlook the wisdom found in Proverbs 3:5-6, which advises us to "Trust in the Lord with all your heart and lean not on your own understanding; in all your ways acknowledge Him, and He will make your paths straight."

Moreover, God reminds us that our struggle is not against our neighbors, colleagues, or loved ones; rather, we are contending with principalities and forces that exist beyond our perception. Without God on our side, we are no match for these evil forces that often infiltrate the minds and hearts of others. This was evident when the disciples were unable to cast out an evil spirit from a young man. Only Jesus had the authority and power to do so (Mark 9:14-29).

This situation teaches us an important lesson in leadership. When the disciples later asked Jesus why they could not expel the unclean spirit, He explained that such challenges required prayer and fasting to access the necessary spiritual strength. Similarly, we will encounter issues that require us to pray, fast, and seek God's guidance to address them effectively.

For example, if we examine the great leaders of the Bible, whom we often quote in our sermons or discussions, we see that each maintained a deep, intentional relationship with God. They did not rely on their own understanding or connections; instead, they consistently sought God's counsel and divine guidance when faced with tough decisions. While they recognized their limitations, they depended on God's ultimate and infinite power. In times of trouble, they remained calm, trusting God to lead them as they carried out their responsibilities. Trusting in God is not a sign of weakness; rather, it is an act of faith and wisdom. It reflects courage and reliance on a power that comes from outside this world—directly from God's throne.

For instance, consider Daniel, Shadrach, Meshach, and Abednego, who faced one of the most challenging moments of their lives. Rejecting a direct order from King Nebuchadnezzar, the most powerful king of that time, was not only an act of courage but also a profound demonstration of their unwavering faith in the Lord and Savior, Jesus Christ.

These young leaders were unaware that God would send Jesus to their rescue until they found themselves in the midst of the blazing furnace. While they were in the midst of the fire, Jesus was with them (Daniel 3:16-28). Remember Elisha? The prophet of God knew he was surrounded by an army sent from heaven, yet his servant could only see the forces against them (2 Kings 6:15). Some situations become much lighter and easier to manage when we seek God first and surrender them into His hands. At times, only you may witness and experience the power of God's divine intervention, leading others to marvel at your leadership style. But always remember—to God be the glory. In all things, give thanks to Him for His guidance.

Although it can be challenging for leaders to take a step back and allow God to lead, there are moments when this is the wisest course of action. We need to learn when to act and when to let God handle things. Failing to do so limits us from being the best leaders we can be, often resulting in more harm than good. This imbalance can increase stress and pain rather than produce peace, making us less productive and fruitful. There is no greater leader than one who walks with God and places their trust in Him.

Remember, the pressures and dilemmas of the world are real. Sometimes, what you do not want or wish for may happen, whether or not you believe in God. Therefore, it is wise to have God on your side, as only He can protect you and help you overcome certain challenges.

Paul expressed, "I can do all things through Christ who strengthens me." He was an exceptional, intelligent leader who faced many difficult decisions, always seeking God's guidance and direction throughout his life. We, too, can emulate the examples set by such leaders—maximizing our potential and demonstrating unwavering leadership. **Attempting to manage life, business, and decision-making without God's presence can lead to unnecessary struggles, create stress for others, and ultimately result in hardship or failure—not only for ourselves but also for those around us.**

Key Takeaways

- Know your enemies, including those that reside within you.
- Remember that some challenges and hardships are designed to make you stronger rather than to harm you.
- Great managers understand their limits and seek guidance, advice, or counsel from trusted and reliable sources—primarily from God.

- Acknowledge that there are some things you cannot accomplish without God's help.
- Divine forces and angels can work on your behalf if you ask, obey, and remain humble.
- Do not ignore or attempt to avoid your problems. Address them promptly while allowing yourself the necessary time to heal.
- Grieving is a natural part of life; how you approach it can make a significant difference in your experience.
- Leaders, too, will encounter inevitable pain and setbacks, but they must position themselves in ways that enable them to bounce back quickly.
- Always seek to solve problems peacefully and with a clear mindset. Never make matters worse.
- Believing in God and relying on His daily provision, strength, and direction is not a sign of weakness; it is, in fact, one of the wisest courses of action.

Chapter 5

Purpose Is The Magic That Makes All Dreams Come True

Purpose First! In this chapter, we will examine why some individuals excel in achieving their dreams while others struggle to make progress in life. We will explore the driving factors that help a person move forward despite setbacks, building incredible resilience, persistence, and endurance to overcome challenges and achieve greatness—even when no one expects it.

One of the most essential factors in life is purpose. A person's management acumen is directly proportional to their objectives or goals. **A life without purpose lacks clear direction.** Such an individual is no different from a cow or a sheep, waiting to be guided, manipulated, and ultimately harmed for the sake of others' greed or profit.

This is why, in many cases, your career is not your true purpose. Many people unconsciously mistake their careers for their purpose, working tirelessly to achieve prestigious positions, only to later discover that—despite their financial success and accumulated fame—they still feel empty, stressed, and miserable. Why is this the case?

Shouldn't you feel happy and stress-free if your bills are paid and your children are well taken care of? How can a person feel unfulfilled despite having many accomplishments? The answer lies in one word: "purpose." Your career can be entirely different from your purpose. **When you**

haven't fulfilled your purpose, you may experience a void or a sense of emptiness, causing you to feel that something is missing.

Our purpose plays a crucial role as the driving force that motivates us to persevere, regardless of the challenges we face. Every person on this planet has been created to fulfill a purpose. But what exactly is purpose? Before we explore this topic further, it's important to understand what purpose truly means, why God gives everyone a purpose, and why it can sometimes be difficult to discover it. In short, purpose is a specific task or calling from God that is uniquely meant for you. No one else can fulfill it quite like you can because God created it specifically for you.

In other words, God created you with a specific mission to serve His people and the world. Every purpose is designed to influence God's creation and its inhabitants in some way. Remember, we are all interconnected; even our small actions can significantly impact the lives of others and create ripples through future generations. Therefore, every purpose given by God is good and intended not only for you but for the entire world. This is why you may feel troubled or empty when you fail to fulfill the order or task God has assigned to you. In essence, the Holy Spirit continually reminds you that something may be missing, encouraging you to seek God's guidance to discover your purpose and accomplish it before you leave this world.

Many people struggle to find their purpose because, although God has a specific mission for each of us, He desires that we accept and fulfill it willingly, without feeling forced. God gives everyone a purpose because He does not want His children to live without value or worth. Most importantly, He wants you to become independent–financially, emotionally, and spiritually–at some point in your life. God's goal is for you to rely on Him as your ultimate source of life. He wants each of His creations to feel valued, important, and worthy.

As a result, God gives you a purpose or a gift, but you should discover or recognize it and make the most of it. He will not force anything upon you. In other words, God will not force you to use the gift or talent he gives you. That is why even though some people find God's gift or purpose in their lives, they still decide not to use it. They'd rather work their entire lives for someone else. Discovering God's gift or purpose for your life does not necessarily mean you will be rich. However, you will be fulfilled and experience lasting joy if you apply it as you should.

Many people struggle to find their purpose because, while God has a specific mission for each of us, He desires that we willingly accept and fulfill it, rather than feeling forced. God gives everyone a purpose because He does not want His children to feel empty or without value. Most importantly, He wants us to become independent—financially, emotionally, and spiritually—at some point in our lives. God's ultimate goal is for us to rely on Him as our source of life. He wants every one of His creations to feel valued, important, and worthy.

God's gift or purpose is designed to provide a sense of fulfillment while supporting and sustaining us. Often, we experience stress and frustration because our lifestyle does not align with the income our gifts or purposes can provide. We may live beyond our means and lack the discipline to refine our gifts, which would allow us to be more fruitful. However, everyone's gift is sufficient to create far more than we can imagine if we use it correctly and wait patiently for God's blessings.

Consider the story of a young man named Allen. He chose to drive his car for nearly twenty years, while most of his friends opted for luxury vehicles. Even when his car made excessive noise, Allen felt no embarrassment. He remained focused on saving his money. Despite being advanced in his career, he answered God's call and embarked on a journey into ministry. How did he know to leave a six-figure salary for one that offered much less? How did he recognize that going into ministry was his true calling?

Though Allen had never considered becoming a minister, he always had a strong love for God. After attending his local church for a few years, his pastor invited him to participate in several services. As he led these services and prayed for the congregation, it became clear to many that he was destined for God's work. He spoke with such sincerity and passion that it felt as though he had been preaching for years. His sermons were so insightful, encouraging, and inspiring that you wouldn't realize he wasn't the pastor unless someone pointed it out.

When you discover your true purpose, it becomes evident that you have a gift or talent for it. While you may not be perfect in delivering that gift to the world just yet, it will come naturally, and others will recognize it.

And the process continued. Many pastors and others who worked with him believed that Allen should enter the ministry. However, Allen refused, as that was not his focus. Despite his career and success, he was not happy; he felt that something was missing. As he searched for meaning and purpose, he finally realized that he truly enjoyed teaching, preaching, and writing sermons. He recognized that not only did he love it, but it also provided him an opportunity to continue learning while staying connected to God.

Once you discover your purpose, the more you try to reject it, the more it will resurface as you interact with others or engage with the world for which it was intended.

But Allen faced a dilemma. He knew that most pastors do not earn much money. To leave his career and pursue his purpose would require him to accept a significant pay cut, and he was not ready to do that.

Therefore, he kept pushing the idea aside, believing that his feelings were merely a distraction. He thought that eventually, he would get over the notion of doing God's work for a living. However, that was not the case. The more Allen tried to focus on his career and personal goals, the more miserable he became, despite his success.

When you discover your purpose, you may encounter challenges that lead you to make excuses for not pursuing it. Nonetheless, the desire to fulfill your purpose can become so overwhelming that you will feel out of place if you don't accept your calling.

Allen struggled with the idea of being a leader for God and felt increasingly guilty, knowing he had the talents to fulfill that role. He faced a difficult decision: whether to leave his career or abandon his purpose. Although he had a family to support, he realized he couldn't serve both God and money. Ultimately, he had to make a decision based on faith, despite the challenges that lay ahead. In that moment, Allen chose to pursue God's work and fulfill his true calling. Although he faced many challenges along the way, he finally felt free and at peace. When you choose to follow your true purpose, you experience a sense of liberation—as if you can finally breathe again. It's a profound feeling that words alone cannot fully capture.

After finally recognizing that he had been bestowed with the gift of teaching for God's work, he decided to further develop his preaching and writing skills. After work each day, he dedicated time to pursue his purpose. Year after year, he steadily improved in his calling, as God provided him with opportunities to practice, grow, and shine. On his days off, he would work on his purpose tirelessly, as if he never felt fatigued. Working on your purpose can sometimes be exhausting, but the joy that comes from pursuing it always outweighs the challenges.

Allen seized every opportunity to teach and preach the word of God. While his friends chose to indulge in various luxuries, he made a conscious decision to save his money and pay off all his debts, including student loans and his mortgage, instead of buying a new car. No one understood his choices or why he opted not to purchase a new vehicle.

A few years later, he had more money and wealth than his friends. Notably, he was happier than all of them because he accepted God's call and wasn't afraid to take a leap of faith to start the work that God called him to do. In contrast, many of his friends still work nine-to-five jobs and often complain about their unhappiness. Meanwhile, the young man is thriving; he has written several books and has no financial problems. Therefore, if we are patient, accept who we are, and embrace the gifts that God provides–while also stopping our competition with others–we can achieve far greater things, leading to a life that is ten times more fruitful and fulfilling.

Moreover, consider Moses, who, although highly educated, possessed an extraordinary gift for leadership; he was truly born to lead. Importantly, God bestowed this gift upon him as part of His purpose so that Moses could guide the Israelites out of Egypt and into the Promised Land. However, despite Moses's education and prior experiences, God felt that he required additional training to become well-prepared for his mission. For many years, Moses worked for Jethro, tending his flocks before God ultimately called him to embark on this challenging and remarkable journey.

Thus, when management and purpose coexist, you have a better chance to influence the world and experience God's ultimate blessings. Additionally, purpose and management must go hand in hand to achieve greatness. Whatever gift God gives you, you must have the discipline to work on it and find ways to make it your only occupation. Ultimately, it can work wonders in your life.

Key Takeaways

- Your career may align with your purpose, but they are different from each other.
- Your destination becomes unclear without a defined purpose.
- Finding your purpose brings happiness, and you may feel lost without it.
- Before making a purchase, consider your long-term goals. Ask yourself, "Did I make the most of this item before replacing it?"
- Remember that some people have less than you, yet they maximize the value of what they have.
- Without patience, life can become harder, and you may achieve less.
- Purpose without discipline or effective life management can lead to frustration and disappointment.
- Your purpose is sufficient to support you and your family if you make the most of it and live within your means.

Chapter 6

Purpose Isn't Just Yours

Having a dream or purpose in life is essential. Discovering your purpose means understanding what God has placed in your mind and heart. Your purpose often guides your feelings and emotions, aligning them with God's plan for your life, especially when you are tempted to pursue something different or contrary to His will. Finding your purpose can be as straightforward as having a clear understanding of what God wants you to achieve.

However, finding your purpose doesn't mean you will instantly see the entire picture of what God has in store for you. **Sometimes, God reveals only the foundation of your dream or purpose, rather than the complete vision. This is often because the big plan God has for us can feel overwhelming or frightening if revealed all at once.** Generally, God's plan for you is divided into many parts, with each segment designed to provide momentum and prepare you for a significant event or milestone in your life.

Some moments in life may be filled with disappointments, while others are full of excitement. Regardless of whether these days are joyful or sorrowful, each experience contributes to the person you are meant to become.

Imagine that God comes to you with a grand plan for your life. As He explains this plan, you realize that it will require you to spend thirteen years in prison or in a state of suffering. You will lose your family, and your life will be filled with bitterness, pain, and struggle. Moreover, you will confront all your fears along this journey. Yet, once everything is over, you will emerge strong like a lion and soar higher than an eagle. The world will come to respect you, and you will experience abundance.

However, you will be killed in cold blood because your influence will impact many lives. The world will love you, but others will hate you. Then, God disappears without providing further details or insights. For many people, this would be a difficult truth to accept. Nevertheless, before all these experiences unfold, God ensures that you are fully prepared to embrace the path He has laid out for you—not by compulsion, but willingly, regardless of the outcome.

Can you imagine how many great pioneers faced immense challenges and even the threat of death to make the world a better place? How might they have felt if God had shown them the complete picture of His plan for them? How would you feel in a similar situation? Would you confront the pain and suffering with courage, or would you run from it? Would you be willing to face your fears to reach the level that God has in mind for you, even if the outcome is difficult and unpleasant? Would you be as motivated as you are now? And most importantly, would you cherish the good times knowing they are fleeting and will soon be gone?

While the message may differ for each individual, there are many valid reasons why God does not reveal the entire plan for our lives. In the face of terrible news, many would plead, "Please, Lord, take this cup away from me, for it is too heavy or painful to bear." Even Jesus experienced this, as His purpose was both significant and painful. Yet, without His sacrifice on the cross, we would still be enslaved to sin. We would not have the salvation and freedom we enjoy now, and life would be profoundly different. We would lack the hope of eternal life that we have today.

Therefore, as we accept His calling, God begins to point and guide us in the right direction. As He continues to work with us, we start to see that God's dream for us is far greater than what we first saw or understood. God seems to operate in this way, so that, along the journey, we can begin to trust Him and believe in Him even more as we exercise our faith and stand our ground despite the challenges.

God wants us to accomplish our purpose so badly that He will go to great lengths for us if we accept His call and start working toward it. He is the God who will empower, strengthen, and protect you until He sees your dream or purpose fulfilled. God never gives us a mission and leaves us alone in the process. Not only will God provide everything we need to carry out the mission, but He is always with us as we journey through it. We see that in many cases throughout history. Remember when Joshua had to complete the mission Moses had begun, which was to lead the Israelites to the Promised Land? Like many of us, Joshua was afraid. He witnessed all the challenges Moses encountered with the people. He knew the job he was called to take on was difficult. God saw Joshua's fear, but God told him to be of good courage. (Joshua 1:9)

Isaiah faced a situation similar to many today when God called him to be a prophet. He was tasked with preaching against the idolatry and corruption of Israel's leaders while proclaiming the coming of the messianic King who would establish God's kingdom. Isaiah's world was not much different from ours in terms of corruption, idolatry, and political and economic turmoil–a world where speaking out against injustice and evil rhetoric could lead to criticism, judgment, or even violence. One can imagine how Isaiah felt in such circumstances. However, God reassured him by saying, "Fear not, for I am with you; be not dismayed, for I am your God; I will strengthen you, I will help you, I will uphold you with my righteous right hand" (Isaiah 41:10). History shows that God has always remained true to His promises.

When God calls a person, He not only provides the strength needed for the task but also equips them with the necessary resources. This was evident when God first appeared to Moses at Mount Horeb in the form of a burning bush, giving Moses the mission to lead the Israelites out of Egypt. Despite Moses expressing doubts about his speaking abilities, God insisted that he take on the mission because God believed in Moses's potential. To encourage him, God promised, "I will provide someone who will speak for you. And I will be with you." As we read in Exodus 4:15-16, God provided Moses with Aaron, his brother, who became a prominent leader among the Israelites.

In most cases, there is no excuse for why God's purpose is not fulfilled in our lives. If God's dream or purpose for you remains unfulfilled, you may feel that something is missing. This can lead to feelings of regret and emptiness, as deep down, you know you have a mission or contribution to make to the world or to God's people that you have not completed. Failing to fulfill God's purpose in your life can result in regret and a sense of failure or disappointment, even if you have achieved success in other areas.

Your sense of purpose should motivate you to rise each day with joy and a smile, regardless of your circumstances. Remember, where you are now is not where you will ultimately end up if you embrace God's plan and purpose for your life. When you enter the workplace, approach it with a smile and a sense of joy, knowing that God has placed you in your current position as a training ground for your future. It is crucial to take every job God gives you seriously, whether big or small. **Just because you may not see how a particular role relates to your goals or future does not mean that God cannot use it in your life.** Keep in mind that God knows the complete plan for our lives, including every detail.

On the other hand, we only know what we see and feel; in most cases, we are unaware of the underlying details. However, rest assured that every challenge God presents to you is part of the training for the mission or purpose He has entrusted to you. Much like the famous movie The Karate Kid, where the young man didn't understand why he was cleaning cars and waxing floors, he later realized that these tasks were essential to his training, giving him the confidence to keep fighting until he won.

Therefore, take your job very seriously. It might be God's training ground right where you are. Learn everything you can about your job and perform it well, so that your entire community recognizes your trustworthiness and care for the business, its people, and the audience or industry it serves.

Remember, even the simplest product, service, or job can have significant meaning to others. Whatever you do, approach it with seriousness, for it is a blessing from God that can keep you occupied, provide for your family, or even help you become financially worry-free. Take your job seriously as you work on your gifts or purpose during your own time. When the time is right, God will either promote you or move you from that position, placing you in a better situation. Our lives can change at any moment because God is in control. He has the power to protect, guide, and elevate us to any position or place He deems appropriate.

Dexter has been a taxi driver for over thirty-five years. He has a beautiful wife and six children. He leads an honest life, attends church regularly, and raises his children well. Some of them have become doctors, police officers, and firefighters. Dexter is always available to help at his local church, as he feels that his calling is to be there for others in need.

After his passing, his children discovered that their dad was a millionaire all along, with a net worth exceeding five million dollars. How did he achieve this? For decades, Dexter invested in the S&P 500, allocating a fixed amount each month to the same ETF. He never bragged about his wealth and chose to live a modest and frugal lifestyle. When his kids needed their first cars for college, he bought them used vehicles instead of new ones. This approach taught his children to value what they have and to take life seriously if they want to achieve more.

Dexter truly believes that being available to help others is his calling. I've known him for almost fifteen years, and I have never seen him unhappy or unwilling to help anyone. He is always comfortable helping others, regardless of their background, ethnicity, or race. He doesn't care what people think of him. Sometimes his wife would ask him to stop being so helpful, but he would continue to offer his assistance anyway.

Due to his kindness and love for helping others, some people have taken advantage of Dexter. However, he doesn't mind because he believes that helping others is his calling. As long as he is alive and able to help, he feels fulfilled. When asked, "Why do you do it? Why do you help some people even when they take advantage of you?" he responds with joy and a gentle smile, "That's okay. They will understand their actions one day. But I hope they remember the kindness. I'm just doing what God would want me to do." Dexter recognizes that his purpose extends beyond his family; it encompasses everyone God places in his path.

As God works on you and prepares you for the tasks and purpose He has in mind for you, He wants you to bless others, including your employer, organization, and family. Take Jacob as an example. God sent him to work for Laban for many years, using that time to shape Jacob's personality and character. During this time, God blessed Laban immensely. In Genesis 30:27, Laban acknowledges God's blessing in his life through Jacob, recognizing that he has prospered because of Jacob's presence. Laban states, "If I have found favor in your eyes, please stay. I have learned by divination that the Lord has blessed me because of you."

This statement reflects the mutual recognition between Jacob and Laban of God's intervention and the positive influence of Jacob in Laban's life.

Similarly, while God sets you up for success, His ultimate goal is to bless others through your preparation. Throughout your time with a company, it may experience years of growth. Contracts that were once difficult to secure may now be granted to your employer. The blessings your employer experiences can be attributed to your presence, hard work, and the divine support they may not always recognize.

Many attribute the success of well-known companies not only to strong leadership but also to employees who embody biblical values such as honesty, kindness, diligence, and service.

A commonly cited example is how frontline employees–including cashiers, cooks, and managers–are trained and encouraged to treat customers with respect, patience, and genuine care. Simple phrases like "My pleasure" or "You're welcome" reflect a servant-hearted mindset rooted in the biblical principle: "Whatever you do, work at it with all your heart, as working for the Lord" (Colossians 3:23).

Often, people overlook the blessings that come from simple acts of service, which can lead to several positive outcomes:

- Customers experience exceptional service and tend to return frequently.
- Trust and loyalty develop even in competitive markets.
- Employees find purpose and accountability beyond just profit.
- The company thrives while upholding ethical standards.

Take Joann, for example. She is a devoted servant of God who works tirelessly for her organization. Always punctual and rarely absent, Joann has positively transformed the work environment since her hiring. Her energy and enthusiasm motivate her colleagues, especially during challenging times. Despite the difficulties the organization has faced among staff, Joann consistently finds ways to keep things running smoothly and helps restore the company's culture to one that is joyful and peaceful.

Although Joann was an excellent employee, she struggled to earn enough to afford the home she wanted. Nevertheless, she was dedicated to giving and never missed her tithes and offerings. Despite aspiring to purchase a house, she lacked sufficient savings for the down payment. However, Joann remained faithful to God, consistently donating 10 percent of her income while maintaining a clear boundary between her personal life and her work.

To her colleagues, she was the most cheerful and amazing person to be around. Her work was always of excellent quality, and her boss had nothing negative to say about her. Joann continued to pray for a blessing, with the goal of purchasing a home the following year, though she had no idea where the money for it would come from.

Before the year ended, her employer raised her salary by more than five percent. Her boss remarked, "You didn't even have to say a word. We have felt blessed since the moment you walked in here. Since you joined us, employee retention has improved significantly, and people seem much happier around you. Furthermore, the contract we've been working hard to secure has finally been approved. We can now serve more than 7,000 families."

Many believers see this as an example of God rewarding dedicated work, where employees view their roles not just as jobs but as a calling to effectively serve others while remaining faithful to God.

This parallels the story of Joseph in Genesis 39, which tells us that Potiphar's household prospered because the Lord was with Joseph. Similarly, modern believers often observe that God's favor flows through employees who demonstrate integrity, patience, and faithfulness. These employees excel in their work not out of fear of losing their jobs or simply for the paycheck, but because they understand their accountability to their own conscience, integrity, and morals. Furthermore, they are motivated by a deep respect for God, who plays a significant role in their sense of responsibility.

These examples illustrate a faith-based perspective. However, this does not imply that success is guaranteed or serves as measurable proof of divine intervention. Instead, it emphasizes a core biblical principle: **God can bless workplaces through the character, obedience, and discipline of individuals within them.**

Therefore, it's important to take your job and purpose seriously. Strive to learn all the management aspects of your role, even if you are not in a management position. Just as someone who is not a professional football player can understand the game and predict outcomes, you can grasp the business's operations and decision-making processes, regardless of your title. Observe how each manager performs their duties, and evaluate them with discernment as if you were an undercover boss. Ultimately, your purpose should be fulfilled not just for your benefit, but so that others may also be blessed through your obedience and diligence.

Key Takeaways

- Finding your purpose will help you see the bigger picture.
- God is always there to support us on our mission.
- You don't need to be perfect to fulfill God's mission or purpose for your life.

- Where you are now is simply a training ground; God has a greater plan for you.
- Don't worry about your current position; God is preparing you.
- Pay attention to the details, as they will be valuable to you later.
- Stay faithful no matter what, and serve with your whole heart.
- Keep your eyes open, learn from the sidelines, and seize the opportunities that come your way.
- Your purpose not only opens doors for you but also creates opportunities and blessings for others.

Chapter 7

You Must Believe, Trust, And Obey

If you practice the principles we discussed in the previous chapter, you will learn a great deal about effective and ineffective management styles and techniques. This preparation will position you well for promotions within the company. Moreover, by being a team player, you will create numerous opportunities to learn different roles and take on others' tasks when they are absent, on leave, or on vacation. It is essential for you to recognize and understand God's plan and training for your life, allowing the Holy Spirit to guide you. Trusting God and allowing Him to lead you is one of the wisest decisions you can make. While you may have an idea of what He wants you to pursue, only He can guide you in the best and most purposeful way possible.

For instance, I never imagined I would become a writer; therefore, I didn't understand the importance of writing hundreds of pages and papers in college. I wasn't sure why I chose philosophy as my major when my primary intention was to pursue a career in mathematics, not writing. Consequently, becoming a skilled writer was never part of my personal plan. Over time, I realized that it wasn't my plan at all, but God's. His purpose for me was completely different from what I wanted. Despite my attempts to avoid His mission—much like Jonah—God ensured that I was prepared for His calling and purpose.

When I finally accepted God's purpose for my life, I had no excuse not to fulfill His work. Although it was challenging for me to get started, God, as He did with many leaders He called, protected me and gave me the courage I needed to begin His mission. If the Lord did it for me and others, He will do it for you as well. Stay in prayer and trust Him. God will help you realize your purpose and accomplish what he has placed on your heart if you remain faithful and do not give up.

Your purpose will serve as a strong motivation for you. It's important to recognize that your purpose is significant enough that you should intentionally allocate time to work on it each day, even if it's just thirty minutes to an hour. While the amount of time you spend on your dream daily is important, consistency is even more crucial. If you can devote more time to your purpose, do so—it will accelerate your progress and help reduce frustration along your journey.

God wants you to succeed and eventually become independent, but He also expects you to act responsibly. Therefore, He encourages you to respect the jobs of others and to appreciate the opportunities He provides for you to support your family. God desires that we work diligently while pursuing His purpose so we can develop strength, character, endurance, and other skills—all without compromising our integrity or that of our employers and colleagues. Ultimately, God wants us to cultivate excellent management skills, enabling us to confidently handle our business, allocate time for our family and spouse, and build a strong relationship with Him, recognizing that He is the guiding force behind it all.

So, how does learning to manage your life support your calling? First, keep in mind that, in most cases, you cannot control others or their schedules, but you can control your own. As a result, staying on top of your habits, feelings, and emotions—despite obstacles—is crucial for success. A well-managed and balanced life is like a smoothly running watermill; just as a beautiful garden needs a gardener, a well-managed life yields greater and more sustainable results. Consequently, those who manage their lives effectively are more likely to see significant outcomes. However, while some people may achieve success without order, they often struggle to maintain or grow what they have built.

Additionally, it can be challenging to pursue your purpose or calling while juggling everything else around you. Therefore, the better you manage your life, finances, character, and environment, the easier it may become to focus on what truly matters. Time management is essential, as you need to dedicate yourself to what is important instead of what is not. Depending on what you feel called to accomplish, you may need to work at it for years before you are fully prepared. Thus, the more structured and manageable your life becomes, the easier it will be to prepare without feeling stressed or overwhelmed.

As you become more serious about achieving your goals or dreams, managing your time and life will become increasingly important. This may require you to create a comprehensive schedule that takes into account every aspect of your life. Maintaining your health and peace of mind should be a non-negotiable priority. Exercise and dedicated prayer time should definitely be included in that plan.

It's important to note the significance of prayer in this context. Becoming an effective leader without a strong prayer life can be challenging. How can you expect the Almighty God to guide you through difficult times if you're not communicating with Him regularly? Life is filled with distractions and challenges, and if you only pray once a day or not at all, it will be tough to overcome certain obstacles. Remember, while God desires our success, the devil seeks our failure. The enemy will do everything in his power to hinder or destroy us.

That said, developing a prayer life is not as difficult as many people think. First, determine if you genuinely want a close relationship with God and to know Him better. Make it your goal to communicate with God daily. Begin by saying a few words of prayer before you go to bed and when you wake up in the morning. Your prayer doesn't need to be lengthy; it can be as simple as thanking God for the day, His protection, and the gift of life itself.

In the morning, you might say, "Thank you, Lord, for waking me up. Please bless me with a great day today. I place my life and family in your hands, and I trust you, Lord. In Jesus' name, I pray. Amen." What matters most to God is not the length of your prayer but whether you speak from the heart and sincerely mean what you say.

As you maintain a consistent prayer routine before bedtime and upon waking in the morning, consider designating a specific time during the day for a quick or short prayer. God values your efforts to stay in communication with Him. In Exodus 20:5, God states, "I am a jealous God." Therefore, He dislikes it when we pray to or give our time to other gods or idols. God delights when we seek Him or communicate with Him.

To help with this, set an alarm for the same time each day as a reminder to offer a few words of prayer. The location is not important—God will hear you wherever you are as long as you pray with a sincere heart. You don't even need to close your eyes. If you find yourself in a situation where you can't move, you can still speak to Him silently or from your heart, and He will hear you.

For example, you might set your alarm for 11:00 a.m. from Sunday to Saturday. When the alarm goes off, take a moment to pause whatever you are doing for a minute or two. You can keep your prayer simple, such as, "Lord, thank you for the day so far. Please help me finish strong. I love you, Lord. Amen."

The blessings stem from the relationship you are building with God. As you continue to talk to Him and acknowledge His presence, your life will gradually change. Over time, you will discover that you are no longer the same person you once were.

Therefore, we must maintain close communication with the one who knows us and our enemies best: God. Throughout scripture and history, many individuals sought God daily in order to cultivate a strong relationship with Him above all else. They understood that through this relationship, not only would God assist them in achieving their dreams and purpose, but they would also gain the gift of eternal life–something money or wealth cannot buy.

These leaders understood that they could never maintain control over their wealth, peace, and joy without God's presence. Nothing can endure when God is removed from the equation. Eventually, whatever you cling to will do more harm than good if God is not involved. Therefore, the visionary leaders we see in the Bible relied on God not just once, but daily.

For instance, the Bible tells us that Daniel prayed at least three times a day (Daniel 6:10). God's presence was undoubtedly with Daniel when his enemies conspired against him and threw him into the lion's den; he suffered no harm and was released, knowing that God was with him and that his prayers were not in vain.

This serves as a reminder for us to pray frequently because when we do, God hears us–even if it doesn't always feel that way. We can take comfort in knowing that God will come to our rescue or send His angels to help us in times of trouble or distress. The consequences of failing to pray–or failing to wait on the Lord–can be significant or even devastating. That is why the Bible instructs us to "wait on the Lord" (Psalm 27:14).

Do you remember the story of Moses? God provided him with clear instructions on how to address the rock to release water. However, Moses did not wait for God's guidance and ended up striking the rock more times than God had instructed, as if He had not given the right command. Some critics believe Moses may have thought he was supposed to strike the rock more times than God instructed, while others argue that he was simply impatient or frustrated with the people.

Moses serves as a valuable example for leaders everywhere, especially for those who believe in God as their Master and Provider.

In most situations, God's instructions are clear. If you ever doubt or do not understand something, it is best to seek clarity from Him. God will provide the answers you need. If you feel pressured or frustrated, it is crucial to wait for His guidance. Failing to do so can lead to significant consequences.

In Moses' case, he was not allowed to enter the Promised Land because of his actions. Can you imagine enduring all the struggles he faced, only to have everything promised to him taken away due to what might seem like a minor mistake or even the actions of others? After years of dedicated service, it must have been incredibly disheartening for Moses to only catch a glimpse of the Promised Land.

Sometimes, what appears to be a minor issue may carry great significance in the eyes of God. This is why we should never compromise God's word or rush into actions when we see signs that tell us to wait, pull back, or stop.

This teaches us that God sometimes wants us to be still and wait on Him. Can we say the same for today's leaders, who live in a world driven by instant gratification? To answer this question, we must consider whether our fast-paced world can change God's mind or nature.

As we know from scripture, God remains the same today as He was yesterday; He does not change. Therefore, if God asks us to wait, we must do so. **We should resist the temptation to think that God has made a mistake. Remember, God does not make mistakes and will not forget His promises or the guidance He provides us along our journey.**

In the case of Moses, his failure to wait and follow God's instructions cost him not only access to the promised land but also his life. As leaders who believe in God, we must practice patience and wait for His guidance, even when others may frustrate us or suggest we take a different path. Is this possible? Absolutely!

Job is a perfect example of a leader who waited for God, despite having every reason to break his alliance with Him. Although Job could not understand the reasons for his suffering and tragedies, he refused to denounce God. He remained faithful and waited until God changed his situation. Even Job's wife asked him to reject God, but Job stood firm in his faith.

As leaders, we may encounter situations where even those closest to us may not provide the right counsel. It is essential to have the discernment to recognize when our lives have shifted and circumstances are no longer the same. We must remember that God is on our side, not against us. Additionally, we need the courage to wait for God to act on our behalf or in our situations.

Therefore, developing a strong management style that includes prayer should be one of your top priorities. By doing so, you will find that your sense of purpose serves as the driving force that keeps you moving forward, no matter the odds or circumstances. Remember, you are not alone–**the Alpha and Omega is with you.**

This chapter emphasizes key themes such as patience, trust in God, prayer, self-control, and obedience. In a world dominated by constant deadlines, quarterly reports, and the demand for instant results, how can we cultivate patience? How do we develop this essential skill to enjoy its long-term benefits and safeguard ourselves?

Every instance that requires us to wait for two minutes or longer offers an excellent opportunity to practice patience. Additionally, you can make it a habit to delay your reactions in most situations, especially those that are important.

Patience is a powerful skill that many people either overlook or don't know how to utilize effectively. It has the ability to compound over time, regardless of the situation. Patience works best when it is combined with time, but both must be intentionally linked to a specific goal, outcome, or system to produce meaningful results. When patience and time are not tied to a purposeful objective, they can often lead to wasted opportunities.

For example, let's say you want to build an emergency fund. If you deposit 200 dollars each month into a high-yield savings account with an interest rate of 3.5 percent, in 30 years, you will have accumulated more than $125,000. If you maintain that same monthly contribution for an additional ten years, without touching the account, your emergency fund could grow to over 206,000 dollars. If you invested the same 200 dollars monthly in an S&P 500 ETF instead for thirty years, you could accumulate about 410,000 dollars. This illustrates that patience is most effective when paired with consistent habits that compound over time.

It's important to note that patience is not just about waiting for your contributions to grow; it also involves the ability to refrain from spending that money on unnecessary things. The capacity to delay gratification and wait patiently for the long term can be extremely beneficial.

Therefore, cultivating patience is essential. It can be applied in various aspects of life, such as at work, in relationships, and in many different situations. Begin practicing patience whenever you have the opportunity.

Before making a decision, take a moment to pause and reflect.

> Ask yourself, "How will this affect me, my family, or my team in the future?"
>
> Consider, "Is there anything I need to do before making this decision?"
>
> When contemplating a significant purchase, think, "Do we really need this? What alternatives are available? How long can I manage without it?"
>
> If you find that every attempt to move a project forward is unsuccessful, take a moment to stop and reflect.
>
> Ask, "Why isn't anything working? What might I be missing? Is this the direction we're meant to take?"

Make sure to take the time necessary to analyze the situation fully before making any decisions, especially when it involves signing long-term contracts that could have penalties or consequences if broken.

Many people make the mistake of rushing into deals without carefully reading the details or consulting their instincts and judgment. They hurry to sign contracts because they fear they may not find a similar deal again, only to discover later that if they had waited a day or two, a better deal could have been available nearby.

Next time you feel pressured to sign a contract, ask yourself, "Can I take a day or two to think it over?" If the answer is no, remind yourself, "If I can't take my time to think about this deal, then it's likely not a good one." Additionally, bring the decision before God and seek His guidance on whether you should proceed or not.

Throughout the Bible, many leaders sought signs from God when they were uncertain about important decisions. Modern leaders can learn from this practice. One notable example is King Jehoshaphat, who faced an impending attack from three kings. Rather than rushing to create a plan, he turned to God for guidance. He candidly admitted his uncertainty, saying, "We do not know what to do, but our eyes are on You" (2 Chronicles 20:12). In the following verses (2 Chronicles 20:15-22), we see how God responded to Jehoshaphat and fought the battle on his behalf. Similarly, when we encounter significant challenges and feel unsure, we should be honest with God about our doubts. By asking for help, we open ourselves up to His support and guidance.

Gideon's story is a perfect example of a leader who experienced uncertainty about whether the angel of the Lord had truly commanded him to fight the Midianites, who were oppressing the Israelites. In his doubt, Gideon sought confirmation from God and asked for a sign to validate the message he had received from the angel. God granted his request (Judges 6:36-40). The signs Gideon requested were neither difficult nor unreasonable. Although God is capable of anything, these signs were sufficient for Gideon to know that God was supporting him.

In our own lives, when we seek a sign from God regarding attending an event, taking action, or making a decision, we should be mindful of how we phrase our requests. This highlights the fact that even when we need reassurance to move forward, God can provide that clarity. While there are times when God wants us to step out in faith, He also desires that we be confident in our actions and decisions. If we require assistance in taking bold steps for His sake—or to protect ourselves and others—He will ensure we know precisely what to do.

Thus, when asking God for a sign before taking action, it's important to focus on realistic requests that pertain to your situation. Instead of asking for something improbable, like a unicorn appearing, try to request specific signs related to the decision you are making. For instance, if you face a crucial decision and are unsure of what to do, you might say, "Please ensure that the key person involved does not attend the event, so I know not to proceed with the deal." By making your requests more precise, you increase your chances of recognizing God's guidance in your situation. Even if God doesn't provide a clear sign, He will still guide you on what to do next. Many leaders seek God's wisdom before making significant decisions, demonstrating the importance of spiritual guidance in critical moments.

Therefore, when uncertain about what actions to take, it's essential to follow a similar approach. Signs can provide helpful guidance, but they should not be the sole basis for your decisions. Instead, they can confirm your direction or decisions and serve as useful supplements. However, they must not replace prayer, wisdom, and scripture. By intentionally taking your time and waiting on the Lord, you are not only safeguarding yourself and your team but also demonstrating strategic thinking. Moreover, you are cultivating one of the most essential skills—patience.

Key Takeaways

- Patience is a superpower; learn to master it.
- Trust in God to guide you through the process.
- Wait on Him, especially during times of frustration.

- Aim to pray consistently throughout your day; this will help you develop a lasting habit, and you may be surprised by the positive results.
- Work on your patience, as it is essential for lasting success.
- Don't hesitate to ask God for help when you're uncertain about what to do.
- Trust God and wait on Him, even when you feel tempted to stop believing.

Chapter 8

Rich Or Not, Be Humble, Listen, And Remain In God's Presence

While God may allow us to reach certain heights or make progress toward our dreams and purposes, it is ultimately our responsibility to continually seek His guidance. The story of Job illustrates this well; he remained patient even when he could not understand the reasons for his suffering. In the end, God rewarded Job with ten times more than he had before. Throughout this journey, Job stayed faithful and never lost sight of God, even in the midst of his wealth and fame.

However, this is not the experience of most leaders. It is easy to remove God from our lives once we achieve specific milestones in our missions or pursuits. Wealth and fame can often become overwhelming, and managing power can be challenging. In these moments, we may take credit for our achievements instead of acknowledging God. Accepting praise without giving glory to Him, or glorifying ourselves rather than God, reveals the dangers of pride that we should strive to avoid.

As you pursue your purpose and strive to achieve your goals or vision, it can become easy to neglect your relationship with God. This often happens when you are not consistently praying for humility and the spirit of a servant leader. It's essential to fear God, regardless of your position or wealth. Proverbs 9:10 states, "For the fear of the Lord is the beginning of wisdom."

As leaders, we must recognize that success can easily distract us from our devotion and commitment to God. What does not belong to us may suddenly start to feel like it is ours. When we are in charge and making decisions, it's easy to believe that all wealth and accolades are our own. However, we can easily disregard God and stop seeking His advice, guidance, or direction.

For example, after attaining wealth or achieving success, many people might think, "Why should I call on God when I have access to the best doctors in the world?" Others might say, "Why seek God when I have all the money I need?" They forget that, no matter how significant their accomplishments or successes are, God remains in control.

Nebuchadnezzar serves as a prime example of this lesson. Samson provides insight into the consequences of using God's power for personal gain instead of its intended purpose. King Solomon illustrates that everything we seek, pursue, and cling to ultimately amounts to vanity. Although God blessed these leaders, at some point in their lives, each chose to take matters into their own hands, disregarding His commandments and guidance. Therefore, we will explore how each of these leaders highlights a unique danger of pride that we can all learn from.

For example, Nebuchadnezzar, the king of the Neo-Babylonian Empire, was the longest-ruling monarch, governing Babylon for approximately forty-three years. His power and significance were so immense that even Daniel and Nebuchadnezzar's dream, highlighted his importance. In this dream, God revealed the extent of the king's power and what would eventually happen to him if he failed to control his pride and arrogance.

Daniel interpreted the dream by saying, "Your Majesty, you are that tree! You have become great and strong; your greatness has grown until it reaches the sky, and your dominion extends to distant parts of the earth" (Daniel 4:22). **At times, God allows us to attain the highest levels of status–such as power, influence, and wealth–as a means of demonstrating not only His greatness and goodness but also what true love and mercy look like in a fallen world.**

For a human being to hold such power for an extended period can lead to the belief that they are a god and that their power will never diminish. Nebuchadnezzar was renowned for his military strength, his conquests over numerous territories, and the expansion of Babylon's influence. However, his pride and self-centered nature caused him to believe that he had achieved this success entirely on his own.

One day, while walking on the roof of the royal palace in Babylon, he admired all that God had allowed him to accomplish. He declared, "Is this not the great Babylon I have built as the royal residence, by my mighty power and for the glory of my majesty?" (Daniel 4:30). In that moment, he forgot about God and the dream he had experienced. God had given Nebuchadnezzar that dream as an opportunity for him to humble himself and repent.

Similarly, God often presents us with chances to repent for our sins, pride, and arrogance. Unfortunately, many of us fail to seize these opportunities until it is too late.

In Daniel 4:27, Daniel advised King Nebuchadnezzar to renounce his sins and wickedness by doing what is right and treating the oppressed kindly. If he did so, God might spare him from the impending calamities and continue to prosper him. However, Nebuchadnezzar refused to acknowledge God and insisted that he was responsible for all his accomplishments. At that moment, God pronounced His judgment just as He had revealed in the king's dream.

According to Daniel 4:31-32, while the words were still on Nebuchadnezzar's lips, a voice from heaven announced, "This is the decree for you, King Nebuchadnezzar: Your royal authority has been taken from you. You will be driven away from people and will live among wild animals; you will eat grass like an ox. Seven periods of time will pass until you acknowledge that the Most High is sovereign over all the kingdoms on earth and gives them to anyone He wishes."

Because of God's amazing love, He kept His promise to King Nebuchadnezzar by restoring him to power after the king sincerely recognized that God is sovereign, holy, and mighty. Nebuchadnezzar finally understood that all he had and accomplished was due to Jehovah. Throughout history, God has brought down several great men and kings because of their arrogance, self-sufficiency, and pride. Many felt that their achievements made them greater than God. And when that happens, God intervenes. The prince of Tyre is another example; God pronounced his judgment as soon as he believed himself to be equal to the Almighty God (Ezekiel 28:2).

Leaders must be cautious about falling into the same trap as Nebuchadnezzar, who faced severe punishment from God for seven years. Imagine losing not only your position and power for that long but also being stripped of your entire kingdom, family, and friends. Picture your life completely ruined for seven years, living in the mud or jungle, surrounded by insects, worms, and other pests.

Leaders must remain humble as God grants them opportunities to achieve their goals, fulfill their purpose, realize their dreams, and bring their vision to life. They should consistently strive to assist those who are less fortunate. Embrace the responsibilities that come from serving God by helping those who cannot help themselves. **The need for support around the world will always be significant enough to keep leaders focused on God. By mismanaging God's resources and neglecting to protect and support His children, we open ourselves up to destruction.**

Samson was blessed with a gift that many men dream of. His gift and purpose were clear; God had equipped and created him for a specific mission. He was given super strength to confront the Philistines on behalf of his people. In the same way, each of us is designed for a unique purpose. Even if you haven't discovered your own gift and mission yet, know that God created you with them in mind. Ultimately, how you choose to use your gift is up to you. God does not dictate your choices; you can use your gift for His glory or for your own purposes.

Your gift is distinct from your purpose, as demonstrated in the case of Samson. God endowed him with superhuman strength, but his purpose was to use that gift to defend the Israelites and defeat the Philistines, who had oppressed them for many years. Instead of fulfilling this mission, Samson used his strength for his own gratification, becoming distracted by women and pleasure–much like many leaders today. He refused to listen to others, behaving as if he knew everything.

By disregarding God's voice, he acted on his own impulses until it was too late. The consequences he faced were severe: he lost his power and was tortured and imprisoned by his enemies. Nevertheless, even in his imprisonment, God granted him a second chance. Samson repented, regained his strength, and ultimately defeated his enemies before his death.

Sexual temptation has long been one of the enemy's most effective weapons. As leaders, we must commit to living godly lives and seek God's strength to resist temptations that can disrupt our efforts, damage our reputations, and undermine everything we have worked for. Samson and

King Solomon serve as cautionary examples of leaders who faltered in their attempts to follow God and fulfill His will. Their struggles with pleasure and sexual desires hindered their ability to serve God faithfully.

According to Scripture, Solomon had seven hundred wives and three hundred concubines. This abundance indicates that King Solomon struggled with contentment and remained unsatisfied despite God's blessings. Although he had a deep relationship with God, Solomon became distracted and began to worship foreign gods. It is tragic that a leader who knew the true God was led astray to worship inferior deities because of ungodly influences. This highlights the dangers of lust, lack of discipline, and the need for self-control.

Solomon, influenced by the women around him, chose to turn away from God, hindering his own progress in fulfilling God's work, and ultimately set the stage for his downfall. Despite his wisdom–granted to him by God–Solomon had the resources, both military and financial, to accomplish God's clear mission. However, his lack of self-control and poor decision-making caused him to drift spiritually from God. Nevertheless, God remained patient with Solomon, allowing him time to repent and return to Him.

The God we serve is truly marvelous. He always gives His children a chance to repent, turn away from their sinful nature, and become the person He has called them to be. While some seize that opportunity, many choose to boldly reject it, continuing in their sins until it leads to great pain or even death.

Controlling oneself in the face of extreme temptations can be challenging for many leaders. As a result, some leaders may find themselves accepting bribes and compromising their beliefs while disregarding God's principles and standards. While it is true that certain temptations can be difficult to resist, prayer and a focus on the ultimate goal can provide the courage needed to resist them, even in challenging times.

Learning to say no to the things that tempt you most can grant you the inner strength that many leaders often lack. The more you overcome these temptations, the stronger you will become, and your life will become clearer. God will provide you with insights that others may not understand. He will set you apart and use you as an example for the world to witness His mighty works in you.

Unfortunately, both godly and ungodly leaders often forget the most important aspect of life that should guide their behavior and submission to God each day: life itself. Leaders, past and present, frequently overlook this fundamental factor that allows them to navigate their daily responsibilities. We tend to take the breath of life for granted, a gift given to us all.

This breath of life, bestowed by the Creator, resides within us; therefore, it does not truly belong to us. Genesis 2:7-9 tells us that after God created man, He breathed into his nostrils, and the man became a living being. Ecclesiastes 12:7 reminds us that when we die, that same breath of life—often referred to as the soul or spirit—returns to God because He is the Owner and Author of it. Consequently, no matter how much wealth or power we may possess, there is one thing we do not control: the breath of life within us.

Therefore, regardless of who you are, you do not control the breath of life within you. Not even the devil can take that breath from you. In fact, the devil exists because he possesses the breath of life, just like we do. Only God has the power over this breath, which He grants to us daily. This is why God is the one who sustains us and determines how long we live.

Furthermore, we must be cautious, as God blesses us with health, peace, and joy. He opens doors that we cannot open and lifts us to heights we never imagined we could reach. Since God is always in charge of life, He watches over every step of His creation or creatures.

Thus, God may allow you to indulge in your sins or disobedience for many years, leading you to believe that everything will always go your way and that no one can touch you. This mindset can create a sense of superiority over others. If you're not careful, you might eventually come to think that you no longer need God in your life. However, when you least expect it, God will intervene, disrupting your misconceptions or false sense of security. When that happens, the consequences will not be pleasant.

It is fascinating when God appears in a person's life. Typically, three outcomes may occur: God may bless that individual, call them to fulfill a mission, or curse and punish them for their misdeeds. God never communicates with a person without providing a directive to follow after that conversation. Therefore, every leader must consider what will occur when God decides to make His appearance in your life. Will the outcome be a blessing, a calling or mission, a curse, or a punishment? The result depends entirely on the choices you make now and on how you live your life today.

It is never too late to repent and change our negative attitudes or behaviors. Failing to do so will only lead to destruction. This book may serve as a warning for you. God communicates with His people in various ways to bring them back to following godly principles and making wise decisions. As a leader, the choice to change and become a great servant of God, regardless of your position or power, is always yours.

Acknowledging God's role in our lives and the plans He has for us should remain at the forefront of our minds. We should use this understanding to help us align our purpose, lifestyle, and management confidence. As we stay focused and faithful, God will guide us and direct our paths in every decision and at every level of our professional lives, as He has promised.

Avoiding the pitfalls that have misled kings and people from all walks of life is challenging, but it is not impossible. It is essential to discipline ourselves and resist the temptations and desires that often lead to chaos. Preparing for what you anticipate can be one of the best defensive strategies. Therefore, identify your temptations and learn everything you can about them, including their effects on you and those around you.

- Ask yourself, "What are my temptations, and how much have they cost me so far?"
- Consider, "Do these behaviors or temptations impact my finances, health, or family?"
- If they do, reflect on, "How do they currently affect me?"
- Lastly, think about, "How will they impact my future?"

Answering these questions truthfully can help you avoid some of the worst mistakes. Our desires can become like gods in our lives if we're not careful. Take Evelyne, for example. Although she was raised by strict, religious parents, she was driven by a desire to experience life on her own terms. She chased attention, pleasure, and approval wherever she could find them. Her relationships were shallow and temporary, but she convinced herself that fulfillment came from being wanted and having fun. Over time, lust began to shape her choices—how she spoke, how she treated others, and how she viewed herself. People became objects to her rather than souls.

As her desires grew stronger, her faith began to fade. Prayer felt unnecessary, and conviction became inconvenient. Evelyne stopped listening for God's voice because it challenged the life she wanted to lead. She told herself she was free, but in truth, she was controlled by the world and materialism.

Eventually, the consequences of her choices caught up with her. Trust was broken, relationships ended, and her reputation collapsed. The loneliness she had been running from finally caught up with her. Sitting alone after losing the people who mattered most, Evelyne realized that lust had promised fulfillment but delivered only emptiness.

At her lowest point, Evelyne prayed—not with confidence, but with sincerity. She acknowledged her weaknesses and asked God for help, not for pleasure. Gradually, change began to take place. Evelyne sought accountability, rebuilt her discipline, and learned to view others with respect rather than desire. Though her cravings didn't disappear overnight, God gave her the strength to make different choices.

God didn't erase Evelyne's past, but He redeemed it. She was given a second chance—not because she deserved it, but because grace is greater than failure. This time, her life was founded on self-control, humility, and faith.

The goal is not to judge but to help you understand how our temptations can evolve into habits. It's important to recognize how these seemingly simple habits may impact you and those around you in the long run if left unmanaged. To address this issue, begin by reflecting on the problem.

- You might consider asking yourself, "Who else is affected by this behavior? What do people think about me because of it?"

- Additionally, ask yourself, "Could this temptation potentially damage my reputation, marriage, or career?"

- Finally, reflect on, "How can I discipline myself so that my temptations do not overshadow my judgment or decision-making?"

One effective approach is to identify when that temptation arises and what triggers it. From there, start creating a plan to stop or prevent it from taking control over you.

If you find that being in a specific environment or experiencing certain feelings trigger your temptations, take note of this. Create a clear plan to combat the temptation each time you sense it is about to arise. Address the root cause of the issue. For example, if someone significantly contributes to your stress or ungodly desires, it's important to manage your exposure to that person. When those feelings emerge, remove yourself immediately from the environment or temptation.

Focus on addressing the sources of your struggles. Avoid that person or situation, set firm boundaries, and engage in activities that bring you peace, courage, and determination to stay on track. This might include listening to uplifting songs or quotes that inspire you to remain steadfast during challenging moments. Additionally, prayer can be a powerful tool when you feel temptation gaining control over you. Ask God for the strength to resist whatever tempts you.

Another action you can take is to remind yourself of your journey and the progress you've made. Acknowledge that God's assistance has been a crucial part of your path or journey; it's the reason you are still standing and breathing today. By practicing gratitude, you are more likely to remain humble. Make an effort to listen to others and don't overlook their feedback, especially from those who love and care about you. This can help you set aside your pride and prioritize what truly matters.

Key Takeaways

- Give praise to God no matter the circumstances.
- Success can be both contagious and dangerous, so ensure it does not consume you or distract you from God and the most essential aspects of life.
- Regardless of your wealth or success, remain humble, listen to others, and treat them with respect.
- Never assume you are too big or powerful for God to reach you. Remember, He is the one who placed you where you are, whether you believe it or not.
- Be aware of your weaknesses and seek help from those who can assist you, but always prioritize seeking God's help above all else.
- God will manifest in your life one day and will respond to your choices–with either blessings or correction.
- Never believe you have reached your peak; there is always room for growth and further learning.
- Discipline your life to overcome your weaknesses and safeguard yourself.
- Lacking discipline in certain areas can undoubtedly become a liability.

Chapter 9

You Own Nothing. You Are Called To Be A Responsible Manager

We never truly own anything, regardless of how much God blesses us. Everything we possess ultimately belongs to God, including the riches of those who do not believe in Him. While we may think we own our wealth and possessions, in reality, God is the true owner of it all. If He chooses to take these things from us, there is nothing we can do to prevent it. Therefore, we must be mindful of the blessings God has given us, such as our homes, wealth, spouses, and children. Whenever we mismanage these gifts, we risk losing them, as God may decide to remove them from our care. Ultimately, God blesses us so that we can be a blessing to others.

One of the best places to start sharing God's blessings is within the family. This setting is ideal for cultivating gratitude, compassion, love, and a dedication to hard work. Demonstrating care for your spouse by taking your marriage seriously can make a significant impact, as God has a plan for the family. Be honest with your partner; building trust will consistently reassure them of your love. Remember, your actions will speak louder than words.

Minimize spending to support each other while saving together. Collaborate to avoid overwhelming one another. It's important to respect each other's boundaries, pet peeves, and dislikes. Challenge one another to grow in various areas of life, such as maintaining a nutritious diet, exercising, and encouraging spiritual growth. This commitment to spiritual development should be the primary obligation for a family that believes in God and prioritizes their Savior.

As a manager, executive director, or CEO, you must decide whether you believe in God and choose to follow Him. As a leader, it's crucial to determine whether you want to be on God's side or not–to be for Him or against Him. This decision is essential! Failing to choose God's way leaves you vulnerable to the enemy's influence. You must take a stand, just as many of God's leaders did. For instance, Joshua made his decision clear to everyone by declaring, "As for me and my house, we will serve the Lord" (Joshua 24:15).

Many people are confused about the order of priorities when managing their families. In every Christian home, God should come first, followed by family, and then your work or occupation. There should be no debate about this! Yes, God calls you to work, but He also calls you to care for the family He has entrusted to you. Your responsibility goes beyond merely providing for them; you need to ensure their emotional, physical, and spiritual well-being is not neglected. If your son is not feeling well, you should be aware of it. If your wife is unhappy, you should notice, and if your family is facing a financial crisis, you should have a plan in place.

The first commandment states, "You shall have no other gods before me" (Exodus 20:3). This means that nothing should take priority in our lives except God. It is important to remember that, regardless of how capable or powerful we may feel, God is ultimately in control, and we do not completely dictate the course of our lives. Whether we like it or not, God determines the length of our lives and governs the forces beyond our control. Therefore, prioritize your life by putting God first, family second, and work third.

If you disagree with this order and believe that family or work should come first, consider Luke 14:26, which states, "If anyone comes to Me and does not hate his father and mother, wife and children, brothers and sisters, and even his own life, he cannot be My disciple." This statement from Jesus may seem strict or harsh, but it emphasizes the importance of prioritizing God above everything else in our lives. This is not a man-made directive; it reflects God's intention for how we should live. We should not allow our ego, desires, or anyone else to dictate that priority. By showing complete loyalty to God, you will experience blessings beyond what you can imagine.

In a family, there are things that can go beyond our control, and it is only through God that we can find care for what we cannot manage ourselves. He allows us to enjoy His blessings and the fruits of our labor. A wise and fair manager understands this principle.

The same God who asks you to put Him first also makes promises that He will never leave or forsake you if you choose to follow Him. He will bless you and your family in ways that exceed your imagination, regardless of whether you are the richest or the poorest person in the world.

God blesses you so that you can share those blessings and encourage others to participate in His work. In doing so, His blessings extend not only to you but also to your family. Those who support your calling and God's mission will also experience blessings. Just as God did for Abraham, He can do the same for anyone who remains loyal to Him. In Genesis 12:3, God says to Abraham, "I will bless those who bless you, and I will curse him who curses you; and in you all the families of the earth shall be blessed."

Therefore, take good care of what God gives you, whether it's financial wealth or a family, as He has the power to take those blessings away or give them to others. Consider this story: Ben had a wonderful family, but his drinking habit ultimately led to a divorce. Over the years, he had many opportunities to stop drinking, but he never took it seriously until it was too late. His ex-wife now has custody of their children and has since remarried. The kids have a new man in their lives whom they call "Father" or "Dad." Because they grew up with James as their stepfather, they barely recognize their biological father, Ben. When he visits or picks them up, the children show little interest in spending time with him. Although he has recovered from his addiction, his life has never been the same because of his past choices.

The main idea is that whatever God provides, if you don't manage it wisely, He can take it away. This concept is illustrated in the story of the talents, where God punished the servant who took his talent for granted and failed to invest it properly. In Matthew 25:14-30, Jesus explains that God gives everyone something to use. Each person receives a certain amount of money to invest or multiply, referred to as talents in the Bible. It's interesting to consider why they are called talents. In reality, God often does not give individuals physical cash or significant capital to begin their entrepreneurial journey or career. Instead, He equips them with specific talents or gifts that can help them achieve financial success.

As the story unfolds, one of the men decided it was better not to use the talent that God had given him. Meanwhile, the others were actively using their talents and creating excellent opportunities, not only for their investor, Jesus, but also for themselves by generating substantial wealth. The story reveals that when they returned to Jesus, those who invested their talents and put them to good use were able to report significant profits. They returned the portion that was due to the Lord without any issues and expressed their gratitude for the opportunity Jesus had given them, appreciating that He took a chance on them when no one else would.

Consequently, the man who did nothing with his talent was rebuked. Why? His excuses were not valid in God's eyes. He showed laziness, a lack of respect for God's gift, and a deficiency in discipline and hard work, which ultimately ruined his prosperity and led God to curse him. The same can happen to us when we fail to use what God gives us properly or for its intended purpose. Through this example, Jesus teaches us that mismanaging God's gifts or blessings can result in losing even more, both spiritually and practically.

It's evident that these men possess the ability to effectively use their talents; however, one of them has consciously chosen not to utilize his gifts. Similarly, it's not that you lack the potential for success or the capability to make the most of what you have. Often, we simply decide not to put in the necessary effort to change our circumstances. Therefore, anyone who truly desires something can work hard enough to achieve it.

Key Takeaways

- Decide whether you are for God or against Him.
- Everything you own belongs to God.
- What you fail to manage well will be taken away.
- Practice gratitude within your home.
- God blesses you so that you can be a blessing to others.
- Be respectful and honest with your spouse.
- You have the right gifts to turn your life around.
- God provides everyone with something to survive or to earn a living.
- Some things are beyond your control, and only God can change them.
- Put God first!

Chapter 10

The One Thing You Don't Have Much Of, Time

You only live once, and time is the only resource that determines how much you leave behind or what you accomplish in this world. Every moment spent wisely is like a seed invested, while every moment wasted is a step away from your purpose–a lost opportunity to sow countless good deeds in the lives of others. Make the most of your time.

Each time you engage in an activity, take a moment to ask yourself, "Am I using this hour wisely? What am I gaining or contributing?"

- Ask yourself, "Am I spending quality time with this friend or person to help them overcome a problem, find peace, or experience joy?"
- Evaluate the situation and the direction of the conversation to assess how your time is being utilized.
- Consider, "Does staying in this conversation make things better or worse?"

The goal is to assess how you engage in discussions and how you spend your time in daily activities. Understanding this will help you determine whether you are using your time wisely, because how you spend your time matters.

What if you were told that, no matter your occupation or responsibilities, you have the time to pursue your dreams, reach your full potential, and fulfill God's purpose for your life? Would you believe it? The truth is—you do.

God has a purpose for each of us and for our families. That's why it's important to use our time wisely and avoid wasting it on activities or tasks that don't align with our goals. To stay focused, make daily plans and set monthly and yearly objectives for both yourself and your family.

It's also important to recognize that your plans may differ from those of your family members. Therefore, take a moment to ask yourself, "Where do I see myself in ten, twenty, or thirty years?" This reflection can help guide your decisions and align your efforts with your long-term vision.

Consider your future by asking yourself the following question about your family: "Where do I see my family in ten, twenty, or thirty years?" Your personal goals might look like this:

> "I want to earn my doctorate by the age of forty-five, or within the next ten years."
>
> "I aspire to be a successful CEO or business owner by the age of fifty or sixty."

Remember that your goals can be personal and tailored specifically to you. **Your goal or purpose is your calling, and it is essential to fulfill it while also communicating with your spouse and caring for your children.**

If God places something on your heart, you can achieve it by managing your time effectively.

God will never assign you a purpose that you cannot fulfill. While your spouse may not always agree with your goals, he or she should still respect your commitment to supporting the family. It is crucial not to let jealousy or external pressures prevent you from pursuing your personal dreams and aspirations, as long as you maintain a solid foundation for your family. With God's help and guidance, you will succeed.

The Bible teaches us, "For as a man thinketh, so is he" (Proverbs 23:7). Additionally, God assures us, "I will never leave you nor forsake you" (Hebrews 13:5). By managing your time wisely, you can turn the impossible into the possible. Remember, you are not alone on this journey—God is with you. He can go where you cannot, touch hearts that you cannot reach, and overcome the limitations you face. **Therefore, partnering with God is the wisest choice one can make.**

The plan for your family is just as important as the goals you set for yourself. Just as you outline your personal aspirations, you should also create a vision for your family. Picture where you want your family to be in ten or twenty years. Here's how you might articulate that vision or plan:

- "I want my family to be spiritually stronger in the next two years."
- "I want my family to deepen their understanding of God this year."
- "We will hold a Bible study every Sunday at 11:00 a.m."
- "I have my kids conduct their Bible study every night before bed."
- "We will pray together at least three times a week."
- "We will attend church every Sabbath."

Let's examine how this concept applies in real life. Take Benjamin, for example. He isn't the most intelligent person you know and lacks many talents. However, he is incredibly disciplined and organized. If you were to walk into his home, you might assume he is wealthy. And indeed, he is—though not in terms of money, but in the discipline and wisdom he has instilled within his household. As the head of the family, his presence and teachings are so impactful that both of his adult children continue to live by the values and discipline he taught them. They are well-educated and grounded in their faith.

Many parents desire their children to be successful and to lead respectful, spiritual lives, yet they often struggle to emulate the practices of people like Benjamin. They find it challenging to maintain a morning devotion, ensure their kids arrive at church on time regularly, and attend most church events. You cannot build a spiritual life if you are uncertain about the values and lifestyle you want to embody.

For Benjamin, it was clear that he wanted his family and children to have a strong spiritual life. He intentionally designed and modeled this for them. For example, it became a tradition to hold Bible lessons almost every Sunday at 11:00 a.m. The kids knew they had to meet Dad in the living room at that exact time. Together, they read the Bible and discussed key points. Benjamin used this opportunity to answer the children's questions about specific controversial issues, helping them understand God's Word and how it applies to their lives.

Every Wednesday, the family gathered to reflect on the week and pray. The goal was not only to strengthen their relationship with God but also to express their gratitude to Him. They used this time to thank God for their week and to pray for any unseen challenges they might face before the week ended. Although there were times when they were unable to conduct their Sunday devotion or Wednesday prayer routine, they remained consistent for the most part throughout the year.

Benjamin's goal was clear. He wanted his family and children to remain in the presence of the Lord for as long as possible, until they went to college or began living independently. He believed this was a fundamental responsibility of every parent. While it's not necessary to hold your kids' hands forever—unless you choose to—it's important to guide them as they grow. Once they reach a certain age, it's fine to let them experience life on their own. However, parents should never stop praying for their children.

To support this goal, Benjamin made a concerted effort to attend church events with his kids. Whether it was Pathfinders' activities or tabling events, they prioritized participating together. By engaging in these activities, the children realized they were not the only family involved. They made friends with others who shared their interests and beliefs, which helped them grow spiritually without feeling odd or out of place. They learned to embrace their identities without needing validation from anyone else.

These routines are essential because they not only strengthen family bonds but also help the entire family grow closer to God spiritually. For example, the son who once hesitated to pray is now leading the family worship service, and their shy daughter is now conducting the program. While these routines may seem minor, they have the power to transform individuals completely. God's people are not meant to be shy or afraid. As you grow both spiritually and socially, you'll find the power and courage to express your thoughts and achieve remarkable things—both for God and for the people you care about in your community.

Additionally, Benjamin ensured that his children took music lessons, insisting that each of them learn to play an instrument. He believed it was essential to provide them with a well-rounded education that extended beyond the traditional school system. To reinforce this, he often volunteered for his children to sing or perform at their church. By the time they were ready for college, the kids had developed remarkable talents in various areas. They were capable of leading parts of the church service, singing special songs, playing the piano, and more. Although his children have grown up and started their own families and careers, they continue to embrace their faith and carry on the traditions their father instilled in them. They witnessed firsthand that, despite the challenges he faced, his efforts were successful.

Thus, deciding how to raise your children is very important. We should recognize the power, wisdom, and blessings that come from providing them with a solid foundation based on the teachings of God. The Bible advises us to "Train up a child in the way he should go; even when he is old, he will not depart from it" (Proverbs 22:6). This means we should do everything we can to raise them well, ensuring we teach them about God's word so they remain grounded in the discipline and spiritual lessons we have instilled in them. **It is our responsibility to play a significant role in our children's lives, helping them grow into responsible and contributing members of society.**

To achieve a spiritual life within the family, you can follow in Benjamin's footsteps or even surpass him, provided you are willing to put in the effort. While this may not be easy for everyone, it is indeed possible, and the rewards can be incredibly significant, yielding amazing results.

Begin by setting specific goals for the family to work toward, as this is essential for spiritual growth and success. Avoid being vague in your objectives. Create a supportive environment that promotes healthy living and a growth mindset. Engage your family in activities that reinforce your moral and ethical beliefs.

Create a positive environment at home that supports your spouse and children—a space they cherish and look forward to returning to, where they can find peace and joy instead of chaos, noise, confusion, stress, and distractions. Aim to reduce these harmful elements in your home as much as possible.

By taking these actions, you are truly demonstrating effective personal and family management. Keep in mind that life won't always be perfect, but creating a loving home where discipline, peace, and growth serve as the foundation for your family, while you pursue your goals, is commendable. Although this is not an easy task, your spouse and children will appreciate your efforts. **A man who can achieve his goals and fulfill his purpose without sacrificing his family's well-being is genuinely fortunate.** Your children should learn how to behave even when you're not around. Additionally, your spouse shouldn't have to face challenges alone while you work toward your aspirations.

Always strive to be present and engage actively in your family's life. Teach, guide, instruct, and demonstrate good behaviors and what it means to have a godly character. If you are the head of the household or the manager of the home, you are called to be the spiritual leader of that space. If you are the mother or wife, you are called to embody wisdom and virtue. Both partners must support each other in these roles. Lead, love, and teach not just one another, but also your children.

Hence, your goals and purpose for yourself and your family should drive you to make every second count. Stay focused on what truly matters, while avoiding anything petty or ungodly. In doing so, keep your eyes on the grand prize that will benefit both you and your entire family.

Moreover, raising a family while making time for your spouse and pursuing your dreams can be challenging. Nonetheless, with a strong mindset, practical management skills, and faith, you can achieve a great deal without feeling overwhelmed.

Therefore, when times get tough, remind yourself of your reasons for working so hard. Your "why" can motivate you to take the next step and help you reach your goals. In essence, it serves as a reminder to manage your time well so you can fulfill your purpose and make your family's dreams a reality. Thus, use your twenty-four hours wisely to ensure that every second counts!

Key Takeaways

- Everything ultimately belongs to God, including your life and your wealth.
- You are always a manager, and God is the boss, whether you accept this truth or not.
- Show love and respect to your spouse.
- It is important to manage God's blessings and resources wisely.
- Use your time effectively, and you will find the time you need to work toward your purpose and dreams.
- Put God first, as your loyalty to Him is essential.
- Fulfilling your purpose is a priority, no matter the challenges you face.
- Set specific goals for yourself and your family, and keep your focus on the prize at all times.

Chapter 11

Focus And Discipline Are Your Superpowers

In most cases, achieving success requires a strong sense of focus and discipline. You may reach impressive heights, but without these qualities, there's a good chance you could lose everything you've accomplished, and your achievements may not last. Essentially, maintaining what you've earned demands a disciplined lifestyle. The greater your focus, the more likely it is that your dreams will become a reality. Focus increases your chances of success and helps keep you on the right path. While it can be challenging to stay focused, distractions are all too easy to fall into. Without focus, even when you know exactly what you need to do, it can be difficult to stay on track.

Let's take Jonah, for example. He was aware of what God wanted him to do and knew the location of the city where he was supposed to deliver the message. However, Jonah refused to go because his eyes, mind, and heart were focused on the wrong ideologies, beliefs, and principles. He believed there was no need for God to save the city of Nineveh. In his mind, the people of Nineveh had already perished or been consumed by their sins, so he questioned why God shouldn't simply destroy them. Jonah saw no hope for a lost generation and, despite having a clear mission and purpose, chose to disobey God's will.

In many ways and situations, we behave like Jonah. We diminish God's power by telling ourselves that there is no hope. We might say, "I can't do this or that because this person doesn't deserve forgiveness." We might also think, "For all I care, they can go to hell." Like Jonah, we sometimes pray for God to harm our enemies instead of forgiving them for the wrongs they have done to us. This behavior goes completely against God's teachings.

On the contrary, Jesus teaches us in Matthew 5:44: "But I say to you, love your enemies, bless those who curse you, do good to those who hate you, and pray for those who spitefully use you and persecute you." He further states in Matthew 5:9 that "the peacemakers shall be called the children of God, and they shall be blessed." But why is this the case? It is because they obey God even when they feel tempted to hurt those who have wronged them. Instead, they adhere to these teachings: "You shall not kill, seek revenge, or bear a grudge, for vengeance belongs to Me," says the Lord (Exodus 20:13, Leviticus 19:18, and Romans 12:19).

"Blessed are the merciful, for they will be shown mercy" (Matthew 5:7). The story of Jonah illustrates his failure to show mercy, which ultimately derailed him and caused him to lose focus on the divine mission he was given. Achieving success requires a strong focus, not only on our clear missions or purposes but also on the dreams and goals that may lack clarity. When you are focused, your attention is directed toward your dreams, God's calling, or your purpose, making it difficult to become distracted or disturbed.

As you pursue your goals, others may perceive you as selfish, self-centered, mean, or antisocial. However, the truth is that you are none of these things; it's crucial for you to know yourself deeply and understand that you are not defined by others' opinions. If you are a kind, caring, and serious person who is focused on your aspirations, embrace that identity. Don't allow others to change you or disrupt your path. Your focus comes from knowing where you want to go and what it takes to get there. Stay true to your course and don't let anyone distract you or deter you from your dreams.

It's important to take your time and energy seriously. Be mindful of your activities, conversations, feelings, and emotions, as these can sometimes catch you off guard and lead you to waste your valuable time and energy on unnecessary distractions. Instead, engage in pursuits that uplift and motivate you to move forward with your dreams.

To maintain energy and focus, you may need to keep conversations brief or speak less, as even minor distractions can easily divert you from your tasks or goals. Evaluate each conversation or situation, and step back when necessary to dedicate your time to pursuing your dreams, purpose, or what truly matters to you. Understand who deserves your attention and who doesn't. Remember, you cannot please everyone. This doesn't mean being unkind; rather, it's about prioritizing your time for activities and people that inspire you and bring you closer to your dreams, goals, or purpose.

Jesus serves as a perfect example in this context. Although He was social and performed many miracles, He never lost sight of His mission. His focus was always on His work: teaching and preaching the gospel of God, strengthening Himself through prayer and fasting, casting out demons, and accomplishing tasks that others, including His disciples, could not. He maintained his focus even in situations where it might seem otherwise.

Many people misunderstand what it means to focus. Focusing does not imply that you cannot enjoy life. It doesn't mean you can't go to the beach or have fun with your kids or spouse. Instead, focus means you do not waste time. Every minute of your time is thoughtfully allocated to things that matter to you—whether that's your family, your business, or your community. For example, if watching a show or movie energizes you and helps you keep going, then it's perfectly fine to do that.

Focus means being mindful of everything you do and approaching it with moderation. Philippians 4:5 says, "Let everything be done in moderation." God doesn't want you to exhaust yourself; He wants you to rest, relax, have fun, and enjoy life as well. As long as you stay focused and disciplined, it's perfectly fine to embrace these moments.

Even Jesus made time for His friends and those He cared about. He attended a friend's wedding, shared meals, and went fishing with His disciples. However, He always maintained His focus. Each of these events was designed to teach us something important. Additionally, God instructed us, "In six days thou shalt labor and do all thy work, but the seventh day is the Sabbath of the Lord" (Exodus 20:9-11). He further emphasized, "In it, thou shalt not do any work, nor thy son, nor thy daughter, thy maidservant, nor thy cattle that is within thy gates" (Exodus 20:10).

Why did God give us such clear instructions? He did so to show us how many days we should work and exert ourselves without feeling guilty. This reminder highlights that rest and worship are also important parts of God's plan. By obeying God's words and taking the necessary time to rest and praise Him, we receive divine blessings. As a result, our thoughts and decisions become clearer, and our overall health, speed, and accuracy improve. Our focus sharpens, allowing us to see things we couldn't before and to understand situations that were previously difficult to grasp.

Focus, rest, and self-care are closely interconnected. Neglecting self-care can lead to burnout. Without sufficient rest, fatigue sets in—something no energy drink can truly fix. Conversely, maintaining a healthy lifestyle helps you maximize your body's benefits and naturally increase your energy levels. Regular exercise and short naps can enhance your energy and concentration more effectively than any energy drink. Therefore, prioritizing the care of your body, mind, and spirit is essential. The more seriously you take these aspects of your life, the more you will benefit from them.

Key Takeaways

- Without focus and discipline, it can be challenging to make progress in life.
- It is often easier to get distracted than to remain focused.
- Believe in yourself, even as you work on your weaknesses.
- Listen to God's guidance and follow His direction.
- Be social and have fun, but always maintain your focus.
- Avoid judging others; instead, show mercy, forgive, and move forward.
- Make time for yourself and your family.
- When you feel the urge to rush, take a moment to pause. Remind yourself that rushing usually makes things worse and leads to more frustration.
- Be patient, relax, and embrace the challenges, but enjoy the journey. Remember, God is always on time, and His timing is always perfect.

Conclusion

Congratulations! You have come a long way. As life continues to present challenges, remember that there is always a brighter side to the story if you are willing to search for it or endure the journey. Life is like a bag with two pockets: one is filled with difficulties and nightmares, while the other contains beauty, goodness, and abundant wealth. Although we don't always know which side we will wake up on, we have the power to change our circumstances, no matter how chaotic the world may seem.

I encourage you to cherish life and make the most of each day. Live as if you have a major deadline to meet because you do - your purpose, your dreams, and your goals are things you cannot afford to neglect in your life or in the world at large.

Remember, despite our challenges, we have a mission. Millions of people around the world are waiting for relief through your gifts, talents, and purpose. We are all connected in some way, and when we each do our part, even a small act of kindness can have a greater impact than you might realize. Therefore, collaborate with others to become your best self, or pursue your goals independently if needed, because reaching your full potential truly matters to the world. Although the journey may not be easy, it is worth the effort! Cultivate patience, for it is the quiet fuel behind great leadership, wealth, and innovation.

Let go of any negativity in your heart, and you'll discover a wonderful sense of comfort and peace. Embrace your unique journey by steering clear of envy and refraining from comparing yourself to others. Instead, pour your energy into your own goals, dreams, and purpose—celebrating the fact that everyone's path is beautifully distinct! Chasing someone else's dream can often lead to unnecessary challenges.

So, focus on finding your true calling and pursue it with enthusiasm! Remember, you're in your own race, and your only competition is with yourself. At the end of the day, ask yourself: Did I embrace my true potential? Did I make the most of my gifts? Can I confidently reflect, "I have run my course," before I rest? These thoughtful questions are vital for us all to ponder, reminding us to live authentically and wholeheartedly. Embrace this journey; it's uniquely yours, and you have what it takes to shine brightly!

Therefore, I urge you to practice self-discipline because, without it, life can be quite challenging and filled with regrets. You may never reach your true potential without it. Be faithful to your commitments and remain consistent until you achieve your goals. However, once you reach your objectives, do not become selfish or complacent; there is still much work to be done. Many people in your community and around the world need your assistance to navigate what we often refer to as the "tough life." Help wherever you can. Remember that if you are where you are now, someone, somewhere, has helped you along the way. And if you can't think of anyone to thank for your success, consider God—He made it all possible!

Be humble and grateful. Remove pride and lust from your heart daily, as they are the destroyers of many people. Ask God for help when you need it, and give Him praise even when things are going well. Remember, you are never too high or mighty for God to reach you or get your attention. Be wise! Always keep in mind that you are merely a manager entrusted by the Master. Let your actions speak louder than your words. Live a life of obedience and honor towards God—a life that exemplifies what a great leader should be for those who need the courage to rise and shine for the Lord as well.

Therefore, write your own story and pace yourself to reach the finish line. Stay focused and work on improving yourself every day and night. The older version of you is always eager to meet the new you, so keep pushing forward! Don't give up.

All you need is one breakthrough. When that moment arrives, the sky is the limit. Keep digging your well; there is water beneath the surface. Once you reach it, it will overflow, bringing you more than you wish for. God is faithful! Stay on track, keep moving forward, and you will get there.

I encourage you to keep learning and working on yourself every day. There is always room for self-improvement, knowledge, and wisdom, and there's always something new to discover. The more we know and the better prepared we are, the less likely we are to be affected by others' decisions or outside events. The best approach is to consistently educate ourselves and strive to become better versions of ourselves as life progresses. As you explore future volumes, you will uncover more truths. Subscribe to our newsletter at WisdomforHeaven.com to be among the first to receive copies of the upcoming volumes as they are released. Thank you for your support, and I wish you all the best!

Author's Biography

Joseph's journey spans from the shores of the Caribbean to those of the United States, where he has experienced the wonders of God in both the world around him and in his own life. Growing up in a family of eight children was not always easy. He witnessed men taking advantage of those who were less fortunate or unable to defend themselves. However, with God's grace, guidance, blessings, and protection, Joseph avoided becoming a victim. For over three decades, he has observed how greed, envy, and violence have shaped our world. Now, as a leader, God has blessed him with valuable insights and wisdom that have helped him overcome numerous challenges and achieve a fulfilling life that many aspire to today.

Joseph is an alumnus of the University of Florida and Nova Southeastern University, where he earned a bachelor's degree in Philosophy and a master's degree in Computer Science and Information Systems. He has taught Physics and Chemistry for over 20 years.

In addition, Joseph is a three-time entrepreneur and serves on various boards. He is a firm believer in the power of continuous learning and growth. He advocates that the more we challenge ourselves, the more we discover about our lives. Joseph encourages everyone to strive to reach their full potential, as failing to do so denies both themselves and those around them the opportunity to share their unique gifts with the world.

Currently residing in New Jersey, Joseph is enriched by the presence of his wonderful wife and sons, who are the center of his world. His commitment to God and family reflects his core values and priorities, adding a personal touch to his professional journey.

Stay in Contact!

Share your experiences of reading this book. Which chapters stood out to you the most? We would love to hear from you. Stay in touch and join our community on X and Instagram.

Visit us @ WisdomForHeaven.com

www.ingramcontent.com/pod-product-compliance
Lightning Source LLC
La Vergne TN
LVHW090615110826
845146LV00001B/393

* 9 7 9 8 9 9 4 0 8 1 0 3 7 *